SUCCESS
at
FIRST
CERTIFICATE

PRACTICE
TESTS

1

with key

R. O'Neill, L. Arthur, S. Menné, R. Nolasco

Oxford University Press

Oxford University Press
Walton Street, Oxford, OX2 6DP

Oxford New York Toronto Madrid Delhi Bombay
Calcutta Madras Karachi Kuala Lumpur
Singapore Hong Kong Tokyo Nairobi Dar es Salaam
Cape Town Melbourne Auckland

and associated companies in
Berlin Ibadan

Oxford and *Oxford English* are trade marks
of Oxford University Press

ISBN 0 19 453246 1
ISBN 0 19 453247 X [with key edition]
© Oxford University Press 1987

First published 1987
Seventh impression 1992

Typeset by Pentacor Ltd., High Wycombe, Bucks

Printed in Hong Kong.

Acknowledgements

The publishers would like to thank Vicki Lywood-Last and Elizabeth Peel for their
contributions to the book.

Some of the material in this book has previously appeared in the *First Certificate
Companion* by Saxon Menné, OUP, 1984.

*The authors and publishers would like to thank the following for permission to
reproduce copyright material:* British Telecom for permission to reprint an extract
from the *International Direct Dialling Booklet*; E.C.M. Haes from *Bulbs for Small
Gardens* (1967) reprinted by permission of Pan Books Ltd., London and Sydney; The
Health Education Council for permission to reprint an extract from *That's the Limit*;
Hammond Innes from *Atlantic Fury* reprinted by permission of Collins Publishers; Erica
Jong from *Fear of Flying* (1974) reprinted by permission of Secker & Warburg Ltd.; The
Landmark Trust for permission to reprint an extract from *The Landmark Handbook*
(1977); David Lodge from *Changing Places* (1975) reprinted by permission of Secker &
Warburg Ltd; Manpower Services Commission for permission to adapt the leaflet *The
Community Programme*; Joy Melville for permission to reprint an article which
appeared in *The Guardian* 13 November 1985; The Open University for a cartoon from
P914 Parents and Teenagers; Southern Water Authority for permission to reprint an
extract from their *Instalments Booklet*; Time Out Ltd. for permission to reprint an
advertisement from 29 April 1987; Ken Tracton from *The BASIC Cookbook* reprinted by
permission of TAB Books Inc.; The Wellington Weekly News for permission to reprint
an article which appeared 6 August 1986.

Illustrations by: Keith Jones Associates, Coral Mula, Nick Sharratt

Location photograph by: James Petrie

*The publishers would like to thank the following for their permission to use
photographs:* Aspect Picture Library; Sally and Richard Greenhill; The Hutchison
Library; Impact Photos; London Express; London Features International; Manpower
Services Commission; Network Photographers; Photo Co-op

INTRODUCTION

ABOUT THE FIRST CERTIFICATE EXAM

The exam consists of five papers:

Paper 1	Reading Comprehension	1 hour	(40 marks)
Paper 2	Composition	1½ hours	(40 marks)
Paper 3	Use of English	2 hours	(40 marks)
Paper 4	Listening	about 30 mins	(20 marks)
Paper 5	Interview	about 15 mins	(40 marks)

The marks given for each paper are a guideline only, as marks are adjusted and weighted to arrive at the final total for the whole exam of 180 marks. The *with key* edition of this book gives a further breakdown of possible marks within each paper. It also gives you the tapescript for the listening tests (Paper 4).

The pass mark for the exam is 100 out of 180 marks. You will be given a letter grade for the exam: Pass grades are A, B and C, and Fail grades are D and E. You are not allowed to use a dictionary during the exam.

HOW TO PREPARE FOR THE EXAM

You can use this practice test book to improve your performance in the exam. Here are some suggestions:

* Use these tests to *diagnose* your weaknesses. Is there a grammar point or a particular kind of exercise which you find difficult? Make sure you give yourself lots of practice in it.

* Try to *time* yourself. Give yourself the experience of working in exam conditions and to the times given in brackets at the top of each paper in the test book. For the listening (Paper 4) play the tape twice only, and give yourself only a couple of minutes between each playing to complete the task.

* Extend your *vocabulary*. If you meet a word you don't know, look it up after you have completed the paper, and make a note too of any nouns, verbs, adjectives, etc. which are connected with the word. This will help you for the vocabulary questions in the Use of English paper but will also build up your 'word-power' in general.

* *Grade yourself* on writing compositions (Paper 2) and doing interviews (Paper 5). In the exam, Paper 2 is usually judged on factors such as vocabulary, grammatical accuracy, fluency and how well the composition achieves its purpose. Paper 5 is usually graded according to six criteria: fluency, accuracy, pronunciation of words, pronunciation of sentences, communicative ability and vocabulary. Try and find someone to practise Paper 5 from this book with. Try to assess your strengths and weaknesses for writing and speaking according to the criteria given. Think about what you can do to improve your performance in Paper 2 and Paper 5.

PRACTICE TEST I

PAPER 1   READING COMPREHENSION   (1 hour)

SECTION A

In this section you must choose the word or phrase which best completes each sentence. **On your answer sheet** *indicate the letter, A, B, C or D, against the number of each item 1 to 25, for the word or phrase you choose.*

1   The film .... several scenes that might upset young children.
    A admits   B involves   C contains   D displays

2   They talked for three days before finally ....to a decision.
    A reaching   B coming   C bringing   D arriving

3   I am not in the least .... about his opinion.
    A aware   B concerned   C interested   D regarded

4   Their aim is to .... up a new political party.
    A strike   B stand   C set   D show

5   I phoned the bank to .... how much money there was in my account.
    A control   B inspect   C test   D check

6   .... he had no money for a bus, he had to walk all the way home.
    A For   B Thus   C So   D As

7   I looked everywhere but I couldn't find .... at all.
    A anyone   B no one   C someone   D somebody

8   It was .... and we had to walk quickly to keep warm.
    A cold   B fresh   C frozen   D mild

9   I do my best to practise the piano every day .... it is difficult sometimes.
    A even   B when   C also   D although

10   Please would you .... me where the railway station is.
    A say   B explain   C tell   D point

4

11 He has been waiting for this letter for days, and at .... it has come.
    A last   B the end   C present   D the finish

12 You asked me to .... you to post that letter.
    A remember   B remark   C remind   D recall

13 He was busy when I phoned but I hung .... until he was free.
    A back   B off   C to   D on

14 It is hot in the day-time but the temperature .... sharply at night.
    A slips   B drops   C descends   D reduces

15 The children threw snowballs at .... on their way to school.
    A themselves   B another   C each other   D their own

16 It happened .... we were asleep last Friday night.
    A during   B for   C while   D since

17 The plate was right on the .... of the table and could have been knocked off at
    any moment.
    A border   B tip   C margin   D edge

18 I am not sure how old he is but he must be .... for 70.
    A going by   B getting up   C getting on   D going off

19 My watch had stopped so I had no way of knowing the right ....
    A hour   B moment   C time   D o'clock

20 I absolutely .... with everything that has been said.
    A agree   B accept   C admit   D approve

21 We're in good time; there's .... to hurry.
    A unnecessary   B no purpose   C no need   D impossible

22 My brother had his camera .... from his car in the office car-park.
    A robbed   B missed   C lost   D stolen

23 The man who lives opposite us sometimes comes .... for a cup of coffee.
    A on   B over   C off   D to

24 She was singing an old Spanish folksong, a favourite of ....
    A her   B hers   C herself   D her own

25 There was a small room into .... we all crowded.
    A which   B where   C that   D it

SECTION B

In this section you will find after each of the passages a number of questions or unfinished statements about the passage, each with four suggested answers or ways of finishing. You must choose the one which you think fits best. **On your answer sheet,** *indicate the letter, A, B, C or D, against the number of each item 26–40 for the answer you choose. Give one answer only to each question. Read each passage right through before choosing your answers.*

FIRST PASSAGE

Until that October I had never even seen Laerg. This may seem strange, considering my father was born there and that I'd been half in love with it since I was a child. But Laerg isn't the sort of place you can visit easily. The small island group is eighty miles west of the Outer Hebrides. Eighty sea miles may be no great distance, but this sea is the North Atlantic and the seven islands are a lonely group standing in the way of the great storms that sweep up towards Iceland and the Barents Sea.

Oddly enough, it wasn't my father who'd made me want to go to Laerg. He seldom talked of the island. He'd become a sailor as a young man and then married a girl from Glasgow and settled down after surviving a shipwreck in mid-Atlantic but losing his confidence in the sea. It was Grandfather Ross who filled our heads with his talk of island history.

This old man with a fierce face and huge hands had been a powerful influence on both my brother Iain and myself. He'd come to live with us when everyone left the island. He had been the only man to vote against leaving when the Laerg Parliament made its decision, and to the day he died he disliked living on the mainland. It wasn't only that he talked endlessly of Laerg; in the years he stayed with us he taught my brother and myself everything he knew about the way to live on that island of rock, sheep and birds.

I'd tried to get there once a long time ago, hiding away on a fishing boat. But on that trip the boat hadn't gone within a hundred miles of Laerg, and then I joined Iain, working in a Glasgow factory. A year in the Navy followed, and then ten years at sea, and after that I had started the thing I had always wanted to do—I began to study as a painter. It was during a winter spent in the Aegean Islands that I suddenly realized Laerg was the subject that most attracted me. It had never been painted, at least not the way my grandfather had described it. I'd packed up at once and returned to England, but by then Laerg had become a tracking station for the new missile developments. It was a closed island, forbidden to unauthorized visitors, and the Army would not give me permission to visit it.

That was the position until October in the following year when a man called Lane came to my house. It was just after ten in the morning that the phone rang, and a man's voice, rather soft, said, 'Mr Ross? My name's Ed Lane. Are you by any chance related to Iain Ross, reported lost when the Duart Castle sank twenty years ago?' 'He was my brother.'

'He was? Well that's fine. I didn't expect to find you that fast. You're only the fifth Ross I've telephoned. I'll be with you in an hour. O.K.?' And he'd rung off, leaving me wondering what in the world it was all about.

I was working on another book cover for Alec Robinson, but after that phone call I'd found it impossible to go back to it. I went into the little kitchenette and made myself some coffee. And after that I stood drinking it at the window, looking out across the rooftops, an endless view of chimneys and TV aerials. I was thinking of my brother, of how I'd loved him and hated him, of how there had been nobody else in my life who had made up for the loss I'd felt at his going.

26 At the time of Ed Lane's telephone call, Mr Ross
   A   had never been to the island of Laerg.
   B   had been to the island of Laerg once.
   C   had some family living on the island of Laerg.
   D   had not wanted to visit the island of Laerg.

27 At the time of Ed Lane's telephone call, who was on the island of Laerg?
   A   Nobody.
   B   A few visitors.
   C   Some islanders.
   D   Army employees.

28 What makes the island of Laerg difficult to get to?
   A   The distance from the mainland.
   B   The Atlantic weather.
   C   It is so rocky.
   D   Boats do not call there.

29 Mr Ross's father settled down on the mainland because
   A   he had been told to move from the island.
   B   his grandfather had voted to leave the island.
   C   he had become afraid of the sea.
   D   his wife came from Glasgow.

30 When Ed Lane telephoned Mr Ross he had recently
   A   obtained the address of Iain Ross's family.
   B   telephoned four other people called Ross.
   C   lost a friend called Ross in a shipwreck.
   D   visited Mr Ross's house whilst he was working.

SECOND PASSAGE

East Somalia's prolonged shortage of rain, which has already caused food supplies to fail and brought unemployment in farming areas, could also affect the production of electricity, and thus reduce the output from the nation's mines. The mining industry, and especially copper mining, uses a huge amount of electricity and is almost completely dependent on the government Electricity Supply Commission. But the Commission has recently asked the mines what would happen if electricity supplies were reduced by ten, twenty or thirty per cent.

The Commission's power stations, which produce the electricity using coal as fuel, are mostly situated near the large coalfields of Eastern Province. But this area has little water so the cooling towers at the power stations have to be supplied with water from elsewhere. The problem now is that water levels in all rivers and lakes have fallen dangerously low and, in some cases, are well below the intake pipes which feed into the pipelines which supply the cooling towers.

In a desperate attempt to solve the problem, engineers are spending some forty million dollars on building a series of small dams across the Haro river. It is hoped that these dams will make the water level at the Malawa Dam rise so that water can then be pumped through a new pipeline to the power stations.

This will take time and it is now the dry season. Very little rain falls before October or November, and, after a shortage which has lasted for four years and is believed to be the worst in two centuries, nobody can say whether the rains will be sufficient.

The amount of electricity and water used by the mines has tended to increase in recent years. The mines, which produce about half the country's export earnings, need electricity in order to pump fresh air through their workings and to drive machines which crush vast quantities of rock. Each mine also has to provide accommodation for as many as three thousand workers.

31 How might East Somalia's lack of rain affect electricity supplies and mining?
 A Copper mines are having to use less electricity.
 B Coal supplies are failing to reach power stations.
 C Electricity supplies to mines may be cut by up to thirty per cent.
 D Copper mines may be unable to pump water by October.

32 Where does the Electricity Supply Commission produce most of its electricity?
 A Along the Haro River.
 B Near the copper mines.
 C At the Malawa Dam.
 D In Eastern Province.

33 The action that the engineers are taking
 A may not help if there is insufficient rain.
 B will become effective towards the end of the year.
 C should get enough water to the mines.
 D will use up a lot of electricity.

34 The engineers aim to
 A change the direction of the Haro river.
 B keep more water at the Malawa Dam.
 C get more water into the Haro river.
 D dig out artificial lakes near the dam.

35 Why are the copper mines important to East Somalia?
 A They train many skilled mechanics.
 B Each mine employs approximately 3,000 people.
 C Their costs and production are rising.
 D They bring in fifty per cent of what the country earns.

THIRD PASSAGE

Operating commands: The following is a list of typical operating (system) commands.

OLD	Loads a previously saved program. The computer may request the name of the old program or file.
NEW	Allows the user to write a new program. The computer may request a name for the program or file.
LIST	Prints the current program.
RUN	Executes the current program.
SAVE, RESAVE or REPLACE	Saves the current program.
UNSAVE, PURGE or SCRATCH	Deletes the current program.
BYE, GOODBYE or SYSTEM	Exit from the program.

Password: Some computer systems (usually large ones) require the user to enter a password to allow use of the computer's facilities. The password may be numbers, an alphabetical string, or a combination of the two. An illegal password will not allow the user to operate or use the computer.

Example

Computer	PASSWORD?
User	JOHN
Computer	READY

In the above example the password was accepted, but in the following a different password is used.

Example

Computer	PASSWORD?
User	PETER
Computer	ILLEGAL PASSWORD, TRY AGAIN PASSWORD?
User	A NAME OR A NUMBER?
Computer	ILLEGAL PASSWORD, TRY AGAIN PASSWORD?

Generally the computer will allow the user three or four tries. After the fourth try, if the proper password has still not been entered, the connection to the terminal is turned off.

36 What are 'operating commands'?
    A   Instructions from the computer to the user.
    B   Instructions from the user to the computer.
    C   Explanations to the user about what to do next.
    D   Procedures to turn the computer off.

37 To get an existing computer program ready for use it is necessary to enter the command
    A   'list'.
    B   'run'.
    C   'old'.
    D   'ready'.

38 An opposite of the command 'save' is
    A   'replace'.
    B   'scratch'.
    C   'new'.
    D   'goodbye'.

39 'Passwords' are entered on a computer in order to
    A   give instructions to users.
    B   request the name of the user.
    C   print the user's required program.
    D   prevent access by users without authority.

40 In the examples given, after two 'password' mistakes
    A   the computer asks the user to try again.
    B   the terminal is disconnected.
    C   the user must exit from the program.
    D   the computer gives the correct password.

PAPER 2 COMPOSITION   (1½ hours)

*Write **two only** of the following composition exercises. Your answers must follow exactly the instructions given and must be of between 120 and 180 words each.*

1 Give an account of a journey you have made which you will never forget.

2 An important person is coming to visit your school or college. You have been chosen to make the speech of welcome. Write the speech you would make.

3 At what age should children leave home? Discuss.

4 You have heard of a three-month expedition exploring a remote island. Write a letter applying to join the expedition. You should make the beginning and the ending like those of an ordinary letter, but the address is not to be counted in the number of words.

(+ optional questions on prescribed texts)

PAPER 3   USE OF ENGLISH   (2 hours)

1   *Fill each of the numbered blanks in the following passage. Use only* **one** *word in each space.*

The job sounded interesting: with a fashion house .... (1) the city centre.

The telephone conversations I .... (2) had with them were relaxed and

friendly, and the letter from the boss had also been a friendly .... (3). He had

invited me to visit the office and join some of them for lunch. The appointment was

.... (4) twelve o'clock.

I naturally thought long and hard about .... (5) to wear. In the fashion

business, of course, you were expected to be smart. The question was .... (6)

to be businesslike, or fashionable. There was something .... (7) to think

about, too. I had to get there .... (8) train and bus. The journey was over two

hours, and that affects the clothes you choose.

In the end, I decided .... (9) wear my most expensive clothes. These

were a pair of boots, a pair of fashion jeans which had cost me a week's salary, a

hand-made sweater and a coat. I was not .... (10) satisfied with my appearance,

but at .... (11) everything was new and expensive.

In fact, I realized .... (12) my arrival that I had chosen exactly the

wrong clothes. The men in the office .... (13) wearing dark suits and ties.

The women were in business suits.

The boss was just .... (14) friendly as his letter had been. We looked

.... (15) the offices, chatted about the business, and finally went out for

lunch. They had chosen a smart restaurant nearby, where the boss was ....

(16) well known. The restaurant manager greeted him .... (17) name. Then

he caught sight of me. He shook his head apologetically, and smiled. Sorry, he said, the house rules were quite .... (18). No one in jeans would be admitted.

I .... (19) the way out, and we started looking for somewhere

.... (20) to eat.

2   *Finish each of the following sentences in such a way that it means exactly the same as the sentence printed before it.*

EXAMPLE: I haven't enjoyed myself so much for years.

ANSWER: It's years *since I enjoyed myself so much.*

a)   The heat was such that I nearly fainted.

It was ....

b)   I'm going to the theatre tomorrow, and I'm really looking forward to it.

I'm really looking   ....

c)   I've never eaten this before.

It's the first   ....

d)   Is it possible to travel to London by coach?

I wonder   ....

e)   It's a pity you didn't tell us about this.

I wish ....

f)   He's getting someone to mend the windows.

He's having   ....

g)   It started to rain at two o'clock.

It has   ....

h)   They made her hand over her passport.

She was ....

i)   I thought it would be better than that.

   It's not ....

j)   I tried to eat the cake, but it was too sweet.

   The cake was ....

3   *The word in capitals at the end of each of the following sentences can be used to form a word that fits suitably in the blank space. Fill each blank in this way.*

   EXAMPLE: My teacher *encouraged* me to take this examination.   COURAGE

a)   We always have a bed ready in the spare room in case visitors arrive ....
                                                                                                                                    EXPECT

b)   The book does not say much about prices, but is very .... about everything else.   INFORM

c)   The government is expected to take .... against the level of unemployment.   ACT

d)   They have added three new songs to the show, which .... it by about fifteen minutes.   LONG

e)   I am looking for a .... gift for an old lady.   SUIT

4   *Make all the changes and additions necessary to produce, from the following sets of words and phrases, sentences which together make a complete letter. Note carefully from the example what kinds of alterations need to be made. Write each sentence in the space provided.*

   EXAMPLE: I/hope/you/reply/my letter/before now.

   ANSWER: *I was hoping you would have replied to my letter before now.*

Dear Mr Jones,

I/write/you/three times/last two months.

a) ....

Also/try/telephone/several times.

b) ....

Each time/find/impossible/get through/you.

c) ....

Afraid/find/attitude/unacceptable.

d) ....

I/feel/this/go on/long enough.

e) ....

Now time/find/solution/the problem.

f) ....

I/therefore/decide/write/this/last letter.

g) ....

If/no reply/end of this week/you/hear from/my lawyers.

h) ....

Yours sincerely

S J Babbett

5   *You are planning a holiday for a group of thirty 15-year-old children, and are deciding what to recommend. Below is a table giving information about four different holidays which are in the right price range.*

Using the information given, continue the three paragraphs below in about 60 words each.

Mountaineering/horse-riding

7 days, 120 kilometres on horseback. Stay at farms overnight. Dramatic mountain countryside, lakes and forests. Quiet, well-trained horses.

Seaside camping park

7 days. Camping on the beach. 1 kilometre from nearest town. Cafeteria and shop. Clean beach, good swimming. Table-tennis tables. Shower room. Sleep 6 to a tent.

Tour of major historical cities

6 days' coach tour of 10 famous historical towns, 5 nights in hotels/guest houses. Guided tours of museums, cathedrals, places of interest.

Children's camp

Activities/computer studies. In a country school. 10/12 to a room. Morning: computer studies; afternoon: football, walks, swimming. Evening activities. All supervised and organized by trained staff.

My first choice would be ....

....

....

....

....

My second choice would be ....

....

....

....

....

I would not recommend ....

....

....

....

....

PAPER 4   LISTENING COMPREHENSION   (about 30 minutes)

FIRST PART

For questions 1–10 complete this advertisement with the help of information from the interview. Be as brief as possible.

Adopt An Animal
at Woodbridge Zoo

Adopt An Animal

Visit your very own animal at Woodbridge Zoo.

Every animal (and there are more than (1)........................) is waiting to be adopted.

Our Adopt An Animal scheme is open to individuals or groups.

Reasons for adopting

The animals are expensive (2)........................ .

Woodbridge Zoo is a registered charity. It needs donations.

How the scheme works

The scheme is based on what it costs to feed an animal for one year.

Each adoption unit costs (3)........................ .

Examples of costs per animal per year

ANIMAL	UNITS	COST
Lion	(4)..................	(5)..................
Elephant	(6)..................	£5200

What you get

For a £30 unit you get:

An adoption certificate.

(7)................................... of the animal.

A complimentary ticket.

(8)................................... on a sign near the animal.

Write to or telephone   Woodbridge Zoo
Queen's Park

Woodbridge   (9)........................

Telephone   (10)....................................

19

SECOND PART

For questions 11–20 tick (✓) whether you think the statements are true or false.

	True	False
11 Jason's computer sounds strange.		
12 Jason watches TV while he eats.		
13 Jason had VIP at birth.		
14 There are 14 known cases of VIP.		
15 Jason has a liquid diet.		
16 Each litre of Jason's food contains 1,000 calories.		
17 Jason has no stomach.		
18 Jason is not strong enough to go to school.		
19 Jason's treatment is very expensive.		
20 Jason's family have paid for all his treatment.		

THIRD PART

For each of the questions 21–25 put a tick (✓) in one of the boxes A, B, C or D.

21   The woman

    A   didn't see a brochure for the Hotel Solara.

    B   wanted to stay in a hotel like the Solara.

    C   didn't like staying in the Hotel Solara.

    D   recommended the Hotel Solara.

A
B
C
D

22   The second hotel was

    A   smaller than the Hotel Solara.

    B   cheaper than the Hotel Solara.

    C   nearer the beach than the Hotel Solara.

    D   bigger than the Hotel Solara.

A
B
C
D

23   One problem with the second hotel was that

    A   it was too personal.

    B   it was near a factory.

    C   it was hard to sleep.

    D   it was a mile from the beach.

A
B
C
D

24   If your hotel is overbooked on arrival, members of the Association of Travel Agents will

    A   send you home immediately.

    B   give you a total refund.

    C   offer you a better hotel.

    D   try to find you another one.

A
B
C
D

25   The expert told the woman

    A   to talk to the tour representative.

    B   that she will get her money back.

    C   to go to the people who sold her the holiday.

    D   to write to his Association first.

A
B
C
D

PAPER 5   INTERVIEW   (15 to 20 minutes)

SECTION A   PICTURE DISCUSSION

You will be given a photograph and asked to talk about it.

Look at one of the photographs above.

a)   Describe the children in the photograph.
     What do you think each child feels?
     What do you think the children are/have been doing?

b)   Talk about the pleasures and problems of bringing up children.
     What makes them happy or sad?
     What causes parents to worry?

SECTION B   PASSAGES FOR COMMENT

You will be given a passage to comment on.

Read one of the following passages and decide

a)   whether you think it is written or spoken.
b)   who is writing or speaking.
c)   what the passage is about.
d)   what you think about the subject.

---

1   We've always made sure that our children lack for
    nothing —— food, clothes, toys etc. —— so I cannot
    understand why my 15-year-old son would want to steal.
    I've noticed a number of things in his bedroom, like
    pencil cases and books that are not his. He has told me
    that they were either lent to him or he's looking after
    them. But now I've found three calculators and some
    other valuable items. I hate to admit it, but I suspect
    he must be taking them from other children at school.
    My husband would be horrified, so I daren't tell him,
    but I'm so shocked and I don't know how to challenge my
    son. Why is he doing it and how can I ask him?

---

2   Well, what's the point of going to university? I mean
    it doesn't help you get a job or anything these days,
    does it? Anyway I'm tired of 13 years of education.
    It's all so boring. I know I might end up unemployed.
    but I'd rather take my chances than sit in classrooms
    for another three years or more. Maybe I'll go abroad
    or something. Travelling and doing any odd job you can
    get is better than sitting around here.

---

3   Don't worry. I'm sure it's only a period he's going
    through. Kids like to look different. Well, we were
    the same when you think back, weren't we? I bet you
    wore mini-skirts and your dad didn't like it. So your
    Michael's dyed his hair red and green and thinks punks
    are wonderful —— give him six months and he'll have
    forgotten all about it.

SECTION C   COMMUNICATION ACTIVITY

You will be asked to take part in an activity with a group of other students or your examiner.

Study these cartoons from a book entitled *Parents and teenagers*.

Be prepared to discuss the following questions.
Would teenagers in your country express similar views? Why? Why not?
Do you think teenagers need discipline? Why? Why not?
What sort of parents do you think teenagers like?

OR

Take part in a role play. Work in a group of three. Each of you will be given a role. You will be given a minute to prepare your role. You will then take part in a discussion to try and solve a family problem.

17-year-old:	You wish to leave home and live in a flat of your own. You know your parents will be upset, but you want to be more independent. You have just started your first job.
Parent:	Your 17-year-old son/daughter wants to leave home and live in a flat of his/her own. You think he/she is too young, could not afford it and would not look after himself/herself properly. You want to persuade him/her to change his/her mind and stay at home.
Family friend:	You want to help your friends with their family problem. The 17-year-old son/daughter wants to leave home and live in a flat. Give advice and make suggestions to help.

PRACTICE TEST 2

PAPER 1   READING COMPREHENSION   (1 hour)

SECTION A

In this section you must choose the word or phrase which best completes each sentence. **On your answer sheet** *indicate the letter, A, B, C or D, against the number of each item 1 to 25, for the word or phrase you choose.*

1 Have I .... you about how Mary is getting on at college?
   A said   B explained   C answered   D told

2 The teachers at the school .... with 'flu one after the other.
   A went down   B went off   C went out   D went under

3 To promote him so quickly you must have a very high .... of his ability.
   A view   B opinion   C idea   D feeling

4 At the end of the day we watch a little television .... going to bed.
   A before   B then   C upon   D during

5 It's a very nice drink; I'm sure you would like it if you .... it.
   A tested   B proved   C tried   surveyed

6 He was born during the war, which would .... him about 50 now.
   A give   B make   C age   D calculate

7 My phone is out of order, which is a ....
   A hurt   B harm   C trouble   D nuisance

8 The noise got .... as the car disappeared into the distance.
   A smaller   B fainter   C weaker   D slighter

9 I had run out of money but luckily I was able to .... enough to get home.
   A lend   B rent   C loan   D borrow

10 .... the weather forecast it will rain heavily later this morning.
    A On account of   B According to   C Because of   D Due to

11 Give her a telephone number to ring .... she gets lost.
    A whether   B in case   C unless   D perhaps

12   I had to be up early the next morning, so I .... myself and left the party.
 A refused   B thanked   C excused   D apologized

13   The .... part of the week is always busy for me.
 A front   B start   C early   D near

14   When you come tomorrow why not .... your brother with you?
 A fetch   B take   C bring   D carry

15   We had to drive carefully because the road was icy in several ....
 A blocks   B places   C pieces   D bits

16   The butcher cut some steak, ... it up and handed it to me.
 A closed   B wrapped   C wound   D strung

17   Clock-making is very .... work which takes years to learn.
 A skilled   B trained   C educated   D unique

18   The smell was so bad that it completely .... us off our food.
 A set   B took   C got   D put

19   He says he has got .... in his stomach.
 A hurt   B aches   C pains   D suffering

20   One .... of this job is that it is near where I live.
 A goodness   B advantage   C pleasure   D preference

21   Don't .... him to arrive early. He's always late.
 A think   B judge   C attend   D expect

22   The hotel receptionist said she would .... what she could do about the dripping
 tap immediately.
 A find   B try   C see   D look

23   He will do the work and then send you the .... for it.
 A sum   B note   C addition   D bill

24   I had a .... , which I couldn't explain, that something terrible was going to
 happen.
 A sense   B thought   C feeling   D view

25   She seems very confident but you .... never judge by appearances.
 A could   B should   C might   D ought

SECTION B

*In this section you will find after each of the passages a number of questions or unfinished statements about the passage, each with four suggested answers or ways of finishing. You must choose the one which you think fits best. **On your answer sheet,** indicate the letter, A, B, C or D, against the number of each item 26 – 40 for the answer you choose. Give one answer only to each question. Read each passage right through before choosing your answers.*

FIRST PASSAGE

Dear David,

Many thanks for your long and interesting letter. What a pity, though, that you had to write about what Jonathan has been up to in it. I must say it seemed to me quite unnecessary. I couldn't of course let Amanda read it, though she kept asking for days. Rather thoughtless of you, dear, wasn't it, because naturally the children are interested in your letters.

You didn't tell me, by the way, that there was a bomb explosion in your office building shortly after you arrived, but I suppose you didn't want to worry us. Were you in any danger? If things get any worse you'll just have to come home, and we'll have to manage without all that money.

By the way, as you didn't answer my question about the washing-machine, I have bought a new one. Fully automatic and rather expensive but it's super.

I heard about the bomb from Mr Zapp. A very curious visit which I must tell you about. He came round the other evening with the book you wanted. It was the most awkward time, about six just as we were about to have dinner, but I felt that I had to invite him in since he'd taken the trouble to bring your book round and he looked rather miserable standing in the wet snow outside the front door wearing waterproof boots and a funny fur hat. He didn't need any persuading—practically knocked me over in his eagerness to get in the house. I took him into the front room for a quick drink, but it was like an iceberg—I don't bother to light a fire in there now you're away—so I had to take him into the dining-room, where the children were just beginning to fight because they were hungry for their dinner. I asked him if he would mind me serving the children their meal while he finished his drink, hoping this would give him the idea that he should leave promptly, but he said no, he didn't mind and I should eat too, and he took off his hat and coat and sat down to watch us. And I mean watch us. His eyes followed every movement from dish to plate to mouth. It was very embarrassing. The children fell strangely silent, and I could see that Amanda and Robert were looking at each other and going red in the face with the effort of trying not to laugh. In the end I had to ask him if he wouldn't like to join us for the meal . . .

Love,

Rosemary

26 Rosemary is writing this letter to David, who
    A   is coming home soon.
    B   is working away from home.
    C   does not think much about the children.
    D   hasn't written home recently.

27 What seems to be happening to David?
    A   He is in continual danger.
    B   Someone is trying to kill him.
    C   He is earning a lot of money.
    D   He is involved in criminal activity.

28 What does Rosemary's attitude towards David seem to be?
    A   She worries about him all the time.
    B   She thinks more about money and the house than about him.
    C   She lets him do what he wants to do, and does not criticize.
    D   She wants him to be involved in decisions about house and family.

29 Why does Rosemary describe Mr Zapp's visit as a curious one?
    A   She found Mr Zapp's behaviour unusual and strange.
    B   She was interested in getting to know Mr Zapp better.
    C   She had never met Mr Zapp before.
    D   Mr Zapp was tense and unhappy.

30 Why did the children go red in the face?
    A   They had been fighting.
    B   They were having difficulty in not laughing.
    C   They were making faces at each other.
    D   It was too hot in the dining room.

SECOND PASSAGE

Bulbs are ideal for new gardeners, including children, because they are easy to plant and they always flower well in their first season. They need comparatively little attention, provided that the soil has been properly prepared, and the place where they are planted is chosen with care. They will last for many years and give you an annual show of flowers that are often so richly coloured or beautifully formed as to be in a class apart from other garden flowers.

However, it is a mistake to buy bulbs without any plan of what effect you really want from them. I have written this book to help in selecting the most suitable bulbs for the typical, small, modern garden of the non-specialist gardener, and have made some suggestions to help readers who may not have had a garden before.

Too many books for beginners tell new gardeners to grow a few 'sensible' kinds of plants and leave the more interesting kinds to adventurous experts. For the first few years of one's gardening life one should, it seems, concentrate on learning simple techniques while admiring the gardens of more experienced neighbours.

In fact, as a learner-gardener you need not fear that your efforts will necessarily show your inexperience, because (and here I give away a most closely-guarded secret), provided the bulbs come from a really reliable source, it is possible to produce as good results in your first year of gardening as in your eightieth. There are some difficult bulbs that will disappoint you, notably some lilies and a few miniature daffodils, but these are often no more attractive than the really easy ones. Therefore, be bold with bulbs; they are a sound investment for any garden.

Never be content to plant the bulbs by themselves. The majority look best when planted among other kinds of plants, because they have unattractive leaves which are thus hidden. There are a few bulbs, such as standard daffodils, which are, however, at their best grown in short grass.

31 Why should new gardeners try growing bulbs?
    A   They are cheap, so a great many can be grown.
    B   Once planted, little after-care is needed.
    C   They will grow anywhere in the garden.
    D   Their flowers get better and better each year.

32 What is this book on gardening about?
    A   Planning an easily maintained garden.
    B   Up-to-date information on new bulbs.
    C   General advice for beginner gardeners.
    D   The choice of bulbs for small gardens.

33 Inexperienced gardeners are often told that they should
    A   experiment with different plants.
    B   ask their experienced neighbours for advice.
    C   learn by visiting other gardens.
    D   plant only a few types of plants.

34 Bulbs are described as an investment because
    A   they go on flowering all summer.
    B   they flower year after year.
    C   the beginner can learn from them.
    D   they make other plants look good.

35 Some lilies and miniature daffodils are different from other bulbs because they are
    A   particularly attractive in colour.
    B   difficult to grow successfully.
    C   disappointing when they flower.
    D   rare and very eye-catching.

THIRD PASSAGE

City College of Technology

General Information

College hours The college is open for classes from 09.00–21.00 from Monday to Friday. During term time, the Enquiry Desk, Ext.102 is open each weekday from 08.45–18.45 (19.00 for the first month of the Autumn and Spring terms), and after that until the close of classes a senior member of the academic staff is on duty in the Office, Ext.230.

Reports Reports on students' progress may be issued at the end of each term.

Parking For safety reasons, no vehicle may be parked on the roadways within the College Grounds. Season tickets for the car parks may be bought from the City authorities.
There is a speed limit of 10 kph on all roadways within the College grounds. Permits for parking motor-cycles, scooters and bicycles, at the rider's risk, may be obtained from the College Enquiry Office.

Dining Room The College Dining Room is open at the following times:
08.30–11.15   Tea Coffee Snacks
11.30–13.30   Lunches
14.45–15.45   Tea Coffee Snacks
16.30–18.30   Evening meals

Accommodation Students seeking accommodation should contact the Accommodation and Welfare Officer, telephone 69371/4 Ext. 54, who is also available for consultation about student welfare problems.

Miscellaneous The playing of musical instruments or sound reproducers within the College or its grounds is prohibited, except for official or approved purposes. Smoking is prohibited, except in the Students' Common Room, the Dining Room (except 12.00–14.00 daily) and in other areas where 'Smoking Permitted' signs are displayed.

Fees Fees are fixed for each year by the Education Committee, and details of fees are often not available until the end of the Summer term. Students applying to the College who wish to gain some idea of fee levels may contact the College, which will be pleased to give details of fees being charged in the current year. At present most full-time students under eighteen (nineteen in the case of students attending GCSE and Foundation courses) do not have to pay course fees.

36 What should you do if you want to ask the staff in the College Office a question at
    20.00 on a Friday evening?
    A   Wait until 08.45 on Saturday.
    B   Wait until 08.45 on Monday.
    C   Dial extension 230 on the telephone.
    D   Go to the Enquiry Desk unless it is the Summer term.

37 Students with bicycles or motor-cycles
    A   can park their bikes at the side of the College roads.
    B   are not allowed to park bikes anywhere in the grounds.
    C   should purchase parking tickets from the City authorities.
    D   must apply to the College Office for permits.

38 On a weekday the first area of the College to open is
    A   the Enquiry Desk.
    B   the classrooms.
    C   the Dining Room.
    D   the Students' Common Room.

39 Students who are in the College Dining Room at 15.00
    A   are not allowed to smoke.
    B   can have something to eat or drink.
    C   are allowed to play musical instruments.
    D   should not be there at all.

40 What information is given about fees?
    A   There are no fees for classes.
    B   Full details are available from the Enquiry Desk.
    C   Full details are available by phone from the Education Committee.
    D   Fees for the coming year are not yet known.

PAPER 2   COMPOSITION   (1½ hours)

Write **two only** *of the following composition exercises. Your answers must follow exactly the instructions given, and must be of between 120 and 180 words each.*

1   What are the advantages and disadvantages of using public transport?

2   You have been asked to talk about your country to an international group. Write the speech you would make to describe some of the most important features of your country.

3   Write a letter to introduce yourself to someone who lives in a country you are travelling to, and who you would like to visit. You should make the beginning and ending like those of an ordinary letter, but the address is not to be counted in the number of words.

4   Write an account of a music or art festival or performance that you attended.

(+ optional questions on prescribed texts)

PAPER 3   USE OF ENGLISH   (2 hours)

1   *Fill each of the numbered blanks in the following passage. Use only* **one** *word in each space.*

Some friends visiting me from the Caribbean remarked .... (1) the tobacco I was smoking. It seemed that the same tobacco was popular in their country, but I was paying four times .... (2) for it than they were. They offered to send me some when they .... (3) home again. I was very grateful, and promised to pay them for it.

Some weeks .... (4) an official letter arrived in a brown envelope. It was from the customs office, informing me that they had intercepted a package with my name and address .... (5) it. The package was found to .... (6) a letter and some contraband: four packets of tobacco. If I wanted the package, I .... (7) have to pay customs duty, tax and a penalty. If they did not hear .... (8) me, they would destroy the package. It was going to turn .... (9) to be rather expensive tobacco, if I paid everything they demanded. On the other .... (10) I had been looking forward to .... (11) from my friends, and wanted to .... (12) the letter, and I could not get the letter .... (13) paying the duty, the tax and .... (14) on. In the .... (15) I sent the money.

A few .... (16) weeks passed, and the package finally .... (17) me. It was covered .... (18) official government stamps and seals. I opened it and took out the letter. It said 'Here's your tobacco. We hope you enjoy it. It's silly paying .... (19) much for it when we can buy it so cheaply here. We'll send you .... (20) four packets next month.'

2　*Finish each of the following sentences in such a way that it means exactly the same as the sentence printed before it.*

　　EXAMPLE:　I haven't enjoyed myself so much for years.

　　ANSWER:　It's years *since I enjoyed myself so much.*

a)　We couldn't go out because the weather was so bad.

　　It was such ....

b)　Six years ago we started writing to each other.

　　We have ....

c)　My brother and I both went to that school.

　　I went to that school and so ....

d)　I'm never going to visit them again.

　　That's ....

e)　She and I had never been there before.

　　Neither ....

f)　No one has ever discussed that question.

　　That question ....

g)　Someone must meet him at the railway station.

　　He ....

h)　She said to us 'Don't be late'.

　　She told ....

i)　I often get up early.

　　I am used ....

j) He was too far away to hear me.

   He was so ....

3 *Complete the following sentences with* **one** *appropriate word connected with the subject of* **shopping**.

   EXAMPLE: We went to the *chemist's* to get some cough mixture.

a) The sports .... is on the fifth floor in this store.

b) The cashier at the .... was very slow, and there was a long queue waiting to pay.

c) For tools and metal things, you should go to a .... shop.

d) I liked the colour of the trousers, but when I tried them on, I found they did not .... me; the legs were too short.

e) This jacket was a particularly good buy, because I bought it in the summer .... , when it was half-price.

4   *Make all the changes and additions necessary to produce, from the following sets of words and phrases, questions which will complete the conversation. Note carefully from the example what kinds of alterations need to be made. Write each sentence in the space provided.*

EXAMPLE:

Diane: I have to go and visit my family this weekend.
George: go/whole weekend?

ANSWER:

George: *Are you going for the whole weekend?*

Diane: No. I'll try and get back on Saturday evening.

George: When/you/leave?

a) .... ?

Diane: On Friday evening, straight after work.

George: go/train/car?

b) .... ?

Diane: I'll be taking the train.

George: mind/I/use/car/Saturday morning?

c) .... ?

Diane: No, that's fine. But don't have an accident.

George: When/ever/I crash?

d) .... ?

Diane: Well, never. But there's always a first time.

George: What/make/think/I/crash?

e) .... ?

Diane: Nothing. It's just that these things can happen.

George: you/not/trust?

f) .... ?

Diane: Yes, of course I do. Forget I said anything about it.

George: Where/leave/car keys?

g) .... ?

Diane: I'll leave them on the table on Friday morning.

George: not/need/Friday?

h) .... ?

Diane: No, I'll take the train to work, and go straight on from there.

5   *Below is the plan of a town showing a space which is free for development, and the suggestions of three groups interested in using the space for their own purposes.*

Using the information given, summarize in four paragraphs the advantages and disadvantages of each scheme and say which you would choose and why. Write about 50 words for each paragraph.

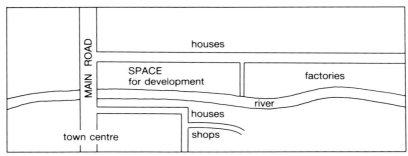

Scheme A
Leisure Interests Ltd.

Build a sports club; squash courts, sauna, gymnasium, small swimming pool. Open to paying members 6 days a week. One day a week available free to schools, hospitals etc.

Scheme B
Acme Supermarkets Ltd.

Build a shopping centre: supermarket, restaurant, banks, with parking for 500 cars. Space on second floor for local shops who want to move there.

Scheme C
Residents' Action Committee

Gardens and riverside walk. Children's playground. Club house by the river for teenagers.

Scheme A: advantages and disadvantages

....

....

....

....

Scheme B: advantages and disadvantages

....

....

....

....

Scheme C: advantages and disadvantages

....

....

....

....

I would choose Scheme .... because ....

....

....

....

....

PAPER 4   LISTENING COMPREHENSION   (about 30 minutes)

FIRST PART

For questions 1–13 complete these notes on the recipe you are about to hear. The information you write should be as brief as possible.

HOW TO MAKE YORKSHIRE PUDDING

Ingredients

You need

① .... grams of flour

② ....

Salt

250 millilitres of ③ ....

One tablespoon of ④ ....

Method

Put flour and teaspoon of salt into bowl.

Remove ⑤ ....

Add ⑥ ...., melted ⑦ .... and half the milk.
Beat the mixture until thick.
Add rest of milk.

Stand until meat is ⑧ .... minutes from being cooked.

Oven must be at ⑨ .... °c.

Put butter or fat into a ⑩ .... cm by 30 cm tin.
Heat tin in oven till it smokes gently.

Pour mixture in. It should make ⑪ ....

Bake in centre of oven for ⑫ ....
Reduce temperature to 200 °c and bake for another 15 minutes.

The pudding should be golden ⑬ .... and well risen.
Serve at once.

SECOND PART

For questions 14 – 22 complete the information about hallmarks. You should be as brief as possible.

(14) System introduced in .... AD was the leopard's head.

(15) Used until ....

(16) Town marks were introduced in .... AD.

A   B   C   D

(17) The town mark for Edinburgh is letter ....

(18) The town mark for Sheffield is letter ....

(19) This is an old mark for ....

(20) This mark shows the silver is ....

(21) This mark shows ....

(22) This mark shows .... It is a letter in a shield.

THIRD PART

For questions 23 – 27 complete these notes made by a member of a group on holiday abroad. The information should be as brief as possible.

(23) Name of the local representative ....

(24) Welcoming drinks in the .... at (25) ....

(26) Dinner tonight at ....

(27) Report for first excursion tomorrow at ....

For questions 28 – 33 tick (✓) whether the following statements are true or false.

	True	False
28 A special excursion has been added to the programme for Tuesday.		
29 The festival celebrates the birth of a poet.		
30 The festival is celebrated with races.		
31 The boatmen saved the poet's life.		
32 People eat fish and rice to remember the poet.		
33 The excursion will take the whole day.		

PAPER 5 INTERVIEW   (15 to 20 minutes)

SECTION A PICTURE DISCUSSION

You will be given a photograph and asked to talk about it.

Look at one of the photographs above.

a) Try to describe the jobs that these people do.
    Do you think they have difficult jobs? Why? Why not?

b) Talk about other dangerous/difficult jobs and the people who do them.

SECTION B PASSAGES FOR COMMENT

You will be given a passage to comment on.

Read one of the following passages and decide

a)   whether you think it is written or spoken.
b)   who is writing or speaking.
c)   what the passage is about.
d)   what you think about the subject.

---

1   I was to start on the Monday, so along I went. They took
    me to the general office and you should have seen the
    mess! There was no floor covering whatsoever, and so
    dusty everywhere. The box files on the shelves were
    falling to pieces and old papers were scattered everywhere.
    The worst shock of all were the tea cups. It was my
    duty to make tea mornings and afternoons. The tea things
    were kept in an old orange-box, and the cups were all
    cracked. After three days I told Mum, and she was upset...

---

2   I find it very difficult to be optimistic...I've applied
    for 130 jobs in the last two years and it's always the
    same story...Come back when you've got a bit of experience.
    I mean, how can I get the experience if nobody wants to
    give me any work? I suppose I shouldn't have left school
    quite so early but I thought it would be easier to get a
    job if I did...I don't know what I'll do.

---

3   SENIOR EXECUTIVES? DIRECTORS. To be or ...?
    Are you going to enjoy your full potential? Are you in
    charge of your future? For help with the answers, come
    and talk to us. We can offer you career advice and help
    in finding the next job.

SECTION C   COMMUNICATION ACTIVITY

You will be asked to take part in an activity with a group of other students or your examiner.

Be prepared to discuss the following topic.
In areas of high unemployment, governments sometimes set up community programmes so that local people can do work which would benefit the community.

Look at the examples of community projects below. Comment on
– the projects that would be most useful to the community you live in.

– a project you would be especially able to help with.

– any projects that you think are a waste of time.

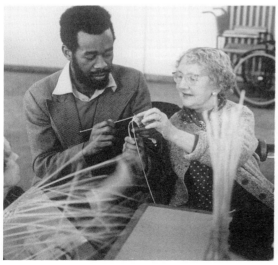

OR

Look at the rules for projects below and devise a community work programme of your own. Present your ideas to the group. Discuss each of the suggestions made. Make sure that each suggestion follows the rules. Choose the best programme.

THE COMMUNITY PROGRAMME

Examples of Projects

Improving the Environment

- Clearing canals and constructing footpaths.
- Tree planting to replace dead trees.
- Creating conservation areas for rare animals and birds.
- Creating picnic areas, nature trails, etc.

Providing Social Amenities

- Creating community centres.
- Providing playgrounds in inner city areas.
- Improving sports facilities for public use.

Helping Local People

- Gardening work for physically handicapped people.
- Running lunch clubs for elderly people.
- Interior decorating service for elderly/disabled people.
- Educational theatre for children in poor areas.

Organizational Guidelines

Basic rules for projects:

1. Projects must be designed to provide jobs which can be done by local people who have been out of work for several months.
2. The work done on projects must be of benefit to the community.
3. Projects should involve work which would not otherwise have been done.
4. Projects involving the production of goods for sale will not be allowed.
5. Projects should not be for work which would normally be done on a voluntary basis.
6. The appropriate 'rate for the job' must be paid to workers on projects.

PRACTICE TEST 3

PAPER 1   READING COMPREHENSION   (1 hour)

SECTION A

In this section you must choose the word or phrase which best completes each sentence.
On your answer sheet, *indicate the letter, A, B, C or D, against the number of each item 1 to 25, for the word or phrase you choose.*

1   The plane crashed into a bridge because it was flying too ....
   A deep   B shallow   C low   D narrow

2   He kept his job .... the manager had threatened to sack him.
   A despite   B unless   C even   D although

3   In order to .... with his studies he worked through the summer.
   A take on   B catch on   C catch up   D take up

4   If you keep trying you might .... to do it.
   A succeed   B discover   C understand   D manage

5   She has to work hard to keep the house .... and tidy with three small children.
   A smooth   B neat   C ordered   D plain

6   He is a little bit .... in his left ear, but if you speak clearly he will hear what you say.
   A disabled   B deaf   C diseased   D dead

7   I am not sure .... the green coat is.
   A who's   B who   C whose   D whom

8   We expected him at eight but he finally .... at midnight.
   A came to   B turned out   C turned up   D came off

9   If you have any .... concerning this report please telephone the Planning Office.
   A queries   B requests   C investigations   D wishes

10 Write to me and tell me .... about your holiday in Switzerland.
   A every   B all   C much   D some

11 She lives near me and I often speak to her on my .... to work.
    A way   B travel   C street   D road

12 He's intelligent but he .... common sense.
    A wants   B fails   C misses   D lacks

13 I shouldn't imagine there is .... on earth who can answer that question.
    A no one   B somebody   C some person   D anyone

14 The hotel has been built on the .... of a lake.
    A border   B boundary   C edge   D front

15 The bill came to over a thousand dollars ....
    A at all   B in all   C to all   D of all

16 The hall was very crowded with over fifty people .... into it.
    A pushed   B packed   C stuck   D stuffed

17 Today's newspaper has .... interesting article on space travel.
    A quite an   B nearly an   C a partly   D an almost

18 The house is in good .... though it needs to be repainted.
    A condition   B state   C position   D standing

19 Tell me .... there is anything special that you would like to do.
    A that   B which   C so   D if

20 The Finance Minister will be making a .... today about new rates of income tax.
    A talk   B notice   C statement   D declaration

21 You need a special .... to go into this part of the building.
    A permission   B allowance   C permit   D agreement

22 The colour of the handle does not .... so long as it is the right size.
    A worry   B affect   C concern   D matter

23 I .... put my money there if I didn't think it was safe.
    A wouldn't   B hadn't   C didn't   D oughtn't

24 We started early .... to miss the worst of the traffic.
    A so that   B in so far   C so long as   D in order

25 He sat there with his arms .... doing nothing, waiting for us.
    A folded   B flapped   C turned   D twisted

SECTION B

In this section you will find after each of the passages a number of questions or unfinished statements about the passage, each with four suggested answers or ways of finishing. You must choose the one which you think fits best. **On your answer sheet,** *indicate the letter, A, B, C or D, against the number of each item 26–40 for the answer you choose. Give one answer only to each question. Read each passage right through before choosing your answers.*

FIRST PASSAGE

My mother always smelled of expensive French perfumes, and she didn't cook much. When I try to summarize the basic lessons she taught me about life, I come up with this:

1 Above all, never be ordinary.
2 The world is a fiercely competitive place: Eat faster!

'Ordinary' was the worst insult she could find for anything. I remember her taking me shopping and the look of scorn with which she would freeze the shop assistants when they suggested that some dress or pair of shoes was 'very popular—we've sold fifty already this week'. That was all she needed to hear.

'No,' she would say, 'we're not interested in that. Haven't you got something a little more unusual?' And then the assistant would bring out all the strange colours no one else would buy—stuff which would have had to be sold off cheaply at sale-time at the end of the season but for my mother. And later she and I would argue fiercely because I wanted to be ordinary as desperately as my mother wanted to be unusual.

'I can't stand that hair-do' (she said when I went to the hairdresser with my friend and came back with a pageboy haircut straight out of *Seventeen* magazine), 'it's so terribly ordinary.' Not ugly; not unsuitable. But ordinary. Ordinariness was something you had to do everything possible to avoid. One way was to repaint and refurnish your house frequently. Actually my mother thought that all the house designers and painters (as well as clothes designers) in America had organized themselves into a spy ring to discover her most recent ideas for houses or dressmaking and suddenly make them popular. And it was true that she had a gift for sensing what would become fashionable (or did I only imagine this?). She painted and furnished the house in antique gold just before antique gold became the most popular colour for curtains and carpets. Then she protested that everyone had 'stolen' her ideas.

She had pink and red towels in the bathroom when pink and red was still considered a very strange colour-combination. Her fear of ordinariness came out most strongly in her clothes.

'Couldn't you please wear something else?' I pleaded when she was dressing for Parents' Day in tight-fitting bullfighter's pants and a bright pink sweater, with a Mexican cape.

'What's wrong with what I'm wearing?'

What wasn't wrong with it!

'It's just that I wish you'd wear something more plain,' I said sheepishly, 'something that people won't stare at.'

She looked at me angrily and drew herself up to her full height of five feet ten inches.

'Are you ashamed of your own mother? Because if you are, Isadora, I feel sorry for you. I really do.'

26 One of the things that Isadora remembers about her mother is
    A the food she cooked.
    B the perfume she used.
    C the way she ate.
    D the magazines she read.

27 What did the shop assistants expect Isadora's mother to want?
    A Something really unusual.
    B Styles they had sold out of.
    C Clothes that were cheap.
    D The most popular clothes.

28 When Isadora had her hair cut in a pageboy hair-style her mother
    A was very angry.
    B disliked it.
    C told her to change it.
    D thought it was childish.

29 As far as fashion and house-furnishing were concerned, Isadora's mother believed that
    A professional designers wanted to copy her ideas.
    B highly fashionable things were best.
    C she would never be in fashion.
    D gold and pink and red were a good colour combination.

30 What did Isadora feel about her mother's clothes on Parents' Day?
    A Afraid.
    B Sad.
    C Embarrassed.
    D Proud.

SECOND PASSAGE

Polyester is now being used for bottles. ICI, the chemicals and plastics company, believes that it is now beginning to break the grip of glass on the bottle business and thus take advantage of this huge market.

All the plastics manufacturers have been experiencing hard times as their traditional products have been doing badly world-wide for the last few years. Between 1982 and 1984 the Plastics Division of ICI had lost a hundred and twenty million dollars, and they felt that the most hopeful new market was in packaging, bottles and cans.

Since 1982 it has opened three new factories producing 'Melinar', the raw material from which high quality polyester bottles are made.

The polyester bottle was born in the 1970s, when soft drinks companies like Coca Cola started selling their drinks in giant two-litre containers. Because of the build-up of the pressure of gas in these large containers, glass was unsuitable. Nor was PVC, the plastic which had been used for bottles since the 1960s, suitable for drinks with gas in them. A new plastic had to be made.

Glass is still cheaper for the smaller bottles, and will continue to be so unless oil and plastic become much cheaper, but plastic does well for the larger sizes.

Polyester bottles are virtually unbreakable. The manufacturers claim they are also lighter, less noisy when being handled, and can be re-used. Shopkeepers and other business people are unlikely to object to a change from glass to polyester, since these bottles mean few breakages, which are costly and time-consuming. The public, though, have been more difficult to persuade. ICI's commercial department are developing different bottles with interesting shapes, to try and make them visually more attractive to the public.

The next step could be to develop a plastic which could replace tins for food. The problem here is the high temperatures necessary for cooking the food in the container.

31   Plastics of various kinds have been used for making bottles
     A   since 1982.
     B   since the 1970s but only for large bottles.
     C   since the 1960s but not for liquids with gas in them.
     D   since companies like Coca Cola first tried them.

32   Why is ICI's Plastics Division interested in polyester for bottles?
     A   The other things they make are not selling well.
     B   Glass manufacturers cannot make enough new bottles.
     C   They have factories which could be adapted to make it.
     D   The price of oil keeps changing.

33   Why aren't all bottles now made of polyester?
     A   The price of oil and plastic has risen.
     B   It is not suitable for containing gassy drinks.
     C   The public like traditional glass bottles.
     D   Shop-keepers dislike re-usable bottles.

34   Manufacturers think polyester bottles are better than glass bottles because they
     A   are cheaper.
     B   are more suited to small sizes.
     C   are more exciting to look at.
     D   do not break easily.

35   Plastic containers for holding food in the same way as cans
     A   have been used for many years.
     B   are an idea that interests the plastics companies.
     C   are possible, but only for hot food.
     D   are the first things being made in the new factories.

THIRD PASSAGE

SOUTHERN WATER COMPANY

PAYMENT

by instalments in eight monthly payments on the 15th day of each month from May to December (inclusive).

by direct debit if you have a bank account, by simply filling in the form enclosed with your water bill and returning it to us within fourteen days. Payments will then be made automatically by your bank on your behalf (and we always tell you in advance the amount and the date on which payment is to be made).

by instalment booklet which will be sent you on completion and return of the slip below within fourteen days. The booklet should be presented with each payment at either a bank or a Post Office or sent with your payment directly to us by post.

Payment by direct debit

Customers are reminded that the direct debit system is not restricted to the eight monthly instalments method of payment.
We consider the direct debit system to be the most efficient and cost effective method of receiving payments – and this system is also available to those making payments annually or half-yearly. Please write or telephone us if you would like to take advantage of this method, and we will send you a special form.
More than two hundred and thirty thousand of our customers already make payment by direct debit (it is cheaper for you than making payment by cheque) and this enables us to keep our administration costs to a minimum.

Request for instalments booklet

Please complete and return within fourteen days to:
Southern Water, PO Box 41, Worthing BN11 1XW

Account number _____

Reference number _____

Name _____

Address _____

36   The direct debit system can only be used for
    A   payments with a special booklet.
    B   all payments through a bank.
    C   payments made within 14 days.
    D   payments made monthly.

37   Customers should complete the section at the bottom of the leaflet
    A   when they pay their bill.
    B   if they want to pay by direct debit.
    C   if they want a booklet to use when paying.
    D   if they are paying their bill within 14 days.

38   What is the advantage of the direct debit system according to the Southern Water Company?
    A   It is quick for people who want to pay in a few days.
    B   Customers do not have to use a bank account.
    C   It is cheaper for the Water Company.
    D   It allows people to pay every month.

39   When you are paying by the direct debit system, Southern Water
    A   will tell you when a payment has been made.
    B   will send you details before a payment is due.
    C   will give you a discount on your water bill.
    D   will not charge you for the months from May to December.

40   The Southern Water Company would prefer people to pay their water bills
    A   by the fifteenth of each month.
    B   within two weeks of getting their bills.
    C   in regular monthly amounts.
    D   through an automatic bank payment system.

PAPER 2   COMPOSITION   (1½ hours)

Write **two only** *of the following composition exercises. Your answers must follow exactly the instructions given, and must be of between 120 and 180 words each.*

1   You are a guest at a friend's birthday party, and are asked to make a speech. Write the speech you would make.

2   Write a letter to someone you met on holiday, explaining that by mistake you still have a record you had borrowed, and saying you are sending the record. You should make the beginning and ending like those of an ordinary letter, but the address is not to be counted in the number of words.

3   Describe a major event or festival that takes place in your home area.

4   Which is your favourite season of the year, and why?

(+ optional questions on prescribed texts)

PAPER 3   USE OF ENGLISH   (2 hours)

1   *Fill each of the numbered blanks in the following passage. Use only* **one** *word in each space.*

Beatrice had had a number of jobs, none of them for very long. She had been a bus

conductor .... (1) one time, then a postman, and then she

.... (2) cleaned the floors in a supermarket. Usually she left the job when

she got tired .... (3) it. Sometimes she was sacked.

   Then one day she saw an .... (4) for a job as a canal warden. She

applied .... (5) the job, just because it sounded interesting,

.... (6) she had no idea what a canal warden did. Surprisingly,

she .... (7) the job, and started work a few days .... (8). As far

as she could see, her duties were to .... (9) an official cap and coat, and

walk .... (10) the banks of the canal, enjoying the fresh air.

.... (11) days when it rained, she would sit .... (12) a cafe nearby,

and watch the canal from there. She .... (13) us it was the best job she had

ever had.

   It was too good to .... (14), of course. One day, she fell into the canal,

and shouted for help. A fellow warden arrived .... (15) find some passers-by

pulling her out. The news that she could not swim .... (16) a shock to her

employers. They said her main purpose was rescuing people .... (17) fell

into the canal. She says she never knew that. She also says they never asked her

.... (18) she could swim. Anyway, she had to start looking for

.... (19) job. She says that she might still have been a canal warden, if it had

not .... (20) for falling in the canal that day.

2   *Finish each of the following sentences in such a way that it means exactly the same as the sentence printed before it.*

EXAMPLE: I haven't enjoyed myself so much for years.

ANSWER: It's years *since I enjoyed myself so much.*

a)   I am sorry I interrupted your dinner.

I apologize ....

b)   Someone stole my purse from my handbag.

My purse ....

c)   'Go home at once, John', she said.

She told ....

d)   It was such good weather that we went swimming.

The weather ....

e)   Getting a good job doesn't interest him.

He ....

f)   The garden is too small to play football in.

The garden isn't ....

g)   When did you start working here?

How long ....

h)   The children should be in bed by now.

It's time ....

i)   No one in the group is younger than her.

She is ....

j)   He can't do anything about it.

      There's ....

3   *Complete the following sentences with one suitable word formed from the word in capitals and* **negative** *in meaning.*

      EXAMPLE: These quantities are *insufficient* for the number of orders received.

                                                                                      SUFFICIENT

a)   I am not saying he is .... , but he's not very good with money.

                                                                                      HONEST

b)   It was quite .... to order so much food.   NECESSARY

c)   You're talking complete ....   SENSE

d)   He seemed to be quite .... about the future.   HOPEFUL

e)   The ending of the detective novel seemed highly ....   PROBABLE

4   *Complete the dialogue.*

Town Information Office, Brighton, Sussex

Tourist: Good morning. Could you suggest what we could visit here? Are there any old buildings, for example?

Officer: Well, there's the Royal Pavilion. It's very famous.

Tourist: (1) .... ?

Officer: Take the number 14 bus from here; it goes straight there.

Tourist: (2) .... ?

Officer: At quarter to and quarter past the hour.

Tourist: (3) .... ?

Officer: Oh, it only takes about 10 minutes, so it's not far.

Tourist: (4) .... ?

Officer: Every day, including weekends. Opening hours are 10am to 4pm.

Tourist: (5) .... ?

Officer: No, not very. It costs £2.00 for adults and 50p for children.

Tourist: (6) .... ?

Officer: Well, why don't you get a family ticket? That's much cheaper.

Tourist: (7) ....

Officer: You're very welcome. Goodbye.

5   *Below is a map of and some information about a village, with three plans for siting a pedestrian crossing there.*

Using the information given, write four paragraphs of 50 words each. In the first three paragraphs outline the advantages and disadvantages of each plan and in the fourth paragraph indicate which one the council should choose, giving your reasons.

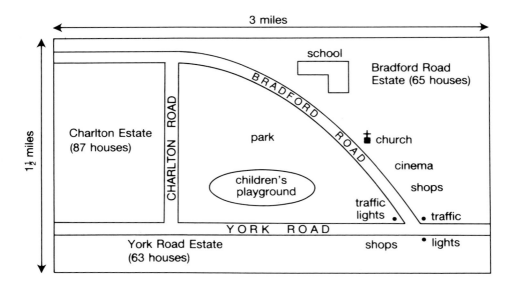

Charlton is a small village of under a thousand people, but two very busy main roads, Bradford Road and York Road, go through the village. This causes traffic problems for the villagers, and for some years they have asked the local council for a pedestrian crossing so that they can cross the roads. The council has agreed to provide one or two crossings with lights and signals. It is now studying three plans and deciding which to adopt.

Plan A: one crossing outside school, across Bradford Road to the park. Cost £4,000.

Plan B: one crossing across York Road, near to Charlton Road. Cost £3,000.

Plan C: two crossings across the junction of York Road and Bradford Road, where the traffic lights now are. Cost £6,500.

Plan A: advantages and disadvantages

....

....

....

....

Plan B: advantages and disadvantages

....

....

....

....

Plan C: advantages and disadvantages

....

....

....

....

I think the council should choose .... because ....

....

....

....

....

PAPER 4   LISTENING COMPREHENSION   (about 30 minutes)

FIRST PART

For questions 1–11 tick (✓) whether you think the statements are true or false.

Winter World

	True	False
1 fixes its prices in advance and does not change them.		
2 has 26 resorts in its brochure.		
3 offers some luxury holidays.		

Olsens

	True	False
4 has skiing holidays for £159 a week.		
5 charges extra for over-55s.		
6 caters for teenagers without their parents.		
7 will give you all your money back if you don't learn to ski.		

Worldwide

	True	False
8 is the largest of the three companies.		
9 gives discounts for late booking.		
10 only offers holidays for the retired.		
11 offers a holiday in a hotel for £2 a day.		

SECOND PART

For questions 12–14 write the information on the appropriate part of the order form.

Question 15 requires you to make four changes on the order form. There is room on the form for six changes. These are lettered a)–f).

*Make the **four** changes required.*

For question 16, write the delivery instructions at the bottom of the form. Be as brief as possible.

OSCARS Sales Note

Order no: (12) ....

Customer's Name: (13) ....

Address: 6, Anville way, Cambridge CB1 5E2

Telephone number: (14) ....

(15)

Description	Code	Price
All items black:		
4 drawer chest	C 6 02631	£ 420
(a) - - - - - - - - - - - - -		(e) - - - - - - - - -
60 cm bedside unit	C 6 02630	£ 160 - 10
Dressing-table top	C 6 02610	£ 90 - 40
	(c) - - - - - - - - -	
220 cm wardrobe	C 6 02618	£ 1,402 - 50
		(f) - - - - - - - - - - -
2 door cupboard	C 36 02692	£ 247 - 50
(b) - - - - - - - - - - - - - - -	(d) - - - - - - - - - -	

Delivery notes:

(16) ....

....

Registered office: Oscar & Son Ltd, 296 New Court Road,
London W3 6FV

THIRD PART

For questions 17–25 complete the information about the boat. Be as brief as possible.

(17)............................. to 1 metre 50 wide.

1 metre 70 to (18)................................. long.

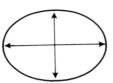

The cow was very important for making coracles.

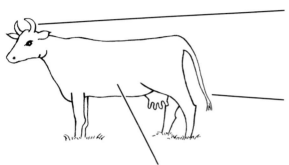

Used to make rings

for the (19).......................................

Used to make

(20)... .

Skin used to cover the (21)........................... frame.

The fat stopped (22)........................... from entering.

Is the correct way to sit A or B? (23)................

A

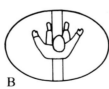

B

Where do the salmon usually swim: A, B or C? (24)................

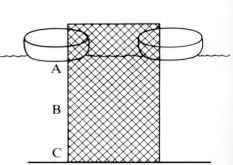

A

B

C

What is the usual distance between the two men? (25)...............................

PAPER 5 INTERVIEW (15 to 20 minutes)

SECTION A PICTURE DISCUSSION

You will be given a photograph and asked to talk about it.

Look at one of the photographs above.

a) What do you think the photograph shows?
Describe the people.
Describe the setting and occasion.

b) Have you ever been to a similar event?
Do you have similar forms of entertainment in your country?
What sort of entertainment do people in your country prefer?

SECTION B   PASSAGES FOR COMMENT

You will be given a passage to comment on.

Read one of the following passages and decide

a)   whether you think it is written or spoken.
b)   who you think is writing or speaking.
c)   what the passage is about.
d)   what you think about the subject.

---

1   It had to happen. You've seen the series so now here's
the record. That's right, <u>Dallas</u>. The record is a
mixed collection of country-and-western tunes with titles
like <u>Who killed Jock?</u>, <u>Lucy's Eyes</u> and <u>JR</u>. For true fans
only.

---

2   Estimates at the end of 1983 suggested that the average
American watched almost 31 hours of television every
week, with most people watching between 8 pm and 11 pm,
followed interestingly by the 10 am to 4.30 pm slot on
Monday to Friday, which just beat the three-hour period
from 4.30 pm to 7.30 pm. Not surprisingly, America has
more TV sets per head of population than any other
country in the world.

---

3   My mother, who also loves the theatre, used to bring me
up to town by bus. Mostly we went to afternoon
performances, so the flashing lights of theatreland are
less a part of my roots than the flower sellers and the
cafés and the theatre buildings themselves. It was the
'going to the theatre' that was special, as much as
seeing a particular play. We always had chocolates and
my mother was careful to make sure they were unwrapped
in advance so that we didn't disturb the people round
us. The theatre is still my hobby as well as my
profession...

SECTION C   COMMUNICATION ACTIVITY

You will be asked to take part in an activity with a group of other students or your teacher.

Look at the advertisements below for films in London cinemas.

Be prepared to discuss the following questions.
Would you want to go and see any of these films? Why? Why not?
Would any of these films be popular in your country? Why? Why not?
What type of films do you like (if any)?

OR

You have decided to use the world of entertainment to draw attention to the problems of a group of people, e.g. the starving in Africa. Your aim is to get as many people to help them as possible. Which of these choices would be the most effective? Which would be the least effective? Put them in order. Put 1 for the most effective, 6 for the least effective and discuss your reasons.

– a play about the problem which is translated into all the major languages
– a specially written pop song
– a world-wide television concert of classical music broadcast by satellite
– a Hollywood film
– a television documentary about the problem, to be shown all over the world
– charity concerts by performers from the affected continent

PRACTICE TEST 4

PAPER 1   READING COMPREHENSION   (1 hour)

SECTION A

In this section you must choose the word or phrase which best completes each sentence. **On your answer sheet** *indicate the letter, A, B, C or D, against the number of each item 1 to 25, for the word or phrase you choose.*

1   The vase is definitely not .... , but just a very good imitation.
    A real   B factual   C genuine   D true

2   You must put your name and address on this side of the form, and then sign on the .... side.
    A back   B other   C opposite   D under

3   The manager expected the team .... because they hadn't done enough training.
    A to lose   B have lost   C to be lost   D by losing

4   Catching the earlier train will give us the .... to do some shopping.
    A opportunity   B luck   C possibility   D occasion

5   This is a photograph of the school I .... when I lived in Swindon.
    A used   B assisted   C joined   D attended

6   .... to an accident in the High Street, traffic is moving very slowly on the London Road.
    A Through   B Owing   C Because   D Since

7   It was .... a simple question that everyone answered it correctly.
    A so   B such   C much   D too

8   The other day I came .... a really beautiful old house in the back streets of Birmingham.
    A across   B over   C by   D down

9   It seems that the world record for this event is almost impossible to............... .
    A meet   B compare   C beat   D balance

10   He could not have known what was in the letter .... he had written it himself.
    A until   B if   C unless   D if only

11 Put the salt in the water and let it .... before adding the vegetables.
 A dissolve   B melt   C soften   D mix

12 I could tell he was pleased .... the expression on his face.
 A at   B for   C in   D by

13 The air in the house felt cold and .... after weeks of bad weather.
 A wet   B moist   C damp   D watery

14 It doesn't sound .... he knows anything about it.
 A that is   B as to   C so as   D as if

15 He took the trouble to write .... the complete list for us.
 A on   B out   C off   D through

16 In her .... she was a famous tennis player.
 A day   B year   C age   D hour

17 One .... of public transport is its unreliability.
 A disappointment   B disadvantage   C disorder   D dislike

18 It is a minor road and very narrow and .... in places.
 A bending   B winding   C wandering   D turning

19 .... from anything else, she is always late for work.
 A Not only   B As well   C Apart   D Except

20 He has a very .... temper and often says things he regrets later.
 A angry   B quick   C warm   D fast

21 Buses into town run .... twenty minutes or so.
 A each   B all   C some   D every

22 He had to go to the bank to .... some money for his holiday.
 A pay up   B pay back   C draw out   D draw in

23 He said he'd come to the meeting .... he might be a little late.
 A although   B even   C whereas   D unless

24 The only way to clean the box is to .... it in soap and warm water.
 A polish   B wash   C brush   D wipe

25 You will have to repeat the course because your work has been ....
 A unpleasant   B unnecessary   C unsatisfactory   D unusual

SECTION B

In this section you will find after each of the passages a number of questions or unfinished statements about the passage, each with four suggested answers or ways of finishing. You must choose the one which you think fits best. **On your answer sheet,** *indicate the letter, A, B, C or D, against the number of each item 26 – 40 for the answer you choose. Give one answer only to each question. Read each passage right through before choosing your answers.*

FIRST PASSAGE

Saddell Castle, 'a fair pile and a strong', was built by the Bishop of Argyll in 1508. By the end of the century it was the house of the Campbell family, who then held it for nearly four hundred years. It is a fine and complete tower-house with a wall-walk round the roof; and it stands at the mouth of a little river, facing the Isle of Arran across a narrow stretch of sea. When we bought it there were small trees growing from the roof, all the windows had gone, and it had not been lived in for many years—indeed it has all but fallen into ruin several times in its long life.

Inside, one bedroom has eighteenth-century woodwork, which was damaged but has now been repaired, and there is a good mid-nineteenth century sitting room. All the windows are set deep into the thick walls and, as usual in such buildings, a number of little cupboards have been hollowed out too. The floor just inside the front door was once removable so that unwelcome visitors could fall straight into a prison below, but it has now been screwed down.

Many Scottish castles and tower-house stand alone. Like that they are impressive, but a good deal less interesting than where, as here, the walls of all the out-buildings survive. The dairy, cattleshed, barn, stable and mill were built at the side of the castle for protection. All the later structural repairs seem to have been a struggle—carried out with whatever was at hand, even poles from old carts, used as door-frames, and lengths of railway track.

Here and there in the castle buildings there are ornamental stones from the ruins of Saddell Church which is a short distance up the valley. On the ground under the trees in that peaceful spot are many gravestones showing wild Scotsmen gripping their long swords or standing in their ancient ships of war—a reminder, as is all Saddell, of Scotland's history, half sorrowful, but half splendid as well.

26 Where is Saddell Castle?
    A   On the Isle of Arran.
    B   By the sea.
    C   In a small wood.
    D   On a rocky hill.

27 What has happened to Saddell Castle over the centuries since it was built?
    A   It has had a series of different owners.
    B   Its owners have looked after it carefully.
    C   It has nearly fallen down several times.
    D   It has remained in much the same condition.

28 What is felt to be interesting about the inside of the castle?
    A   The walls are very thick.
    B   The woodwork was made in the eighteenth century.
    C   The front door can be lifted out.
    D   Several windows have been blocked up.

29 What is thought to be interesting about the outside of the castle?
    A   Bits of old gravestones have been built into the walls.
    B   Several doors are missing.
    C   It is a difficult structure to repair.
    D   The original farm-buildings are still standing.

30 Today Saddell Castle is
    A   in ruins.
    B   someone's house.
    C   a working farm.
    D   part of a church.

SECOND PASSAGE

DRINKING AND DRIVING

The legal limit for driving after drinking alcohol is 80 milligrams of alcohol in 100 millilitres of blood, when tested. But there is no sure way of telling how much you can drink before you reach this limit. It varies with each person depending on your weight, your sex, if you've just eaten and what sort of drinks you've had. Some people might reach their limit after only about three standard drinks.

In fact, your driving ability can be affected by just one or two drinks. Even if you're below the legal limit, you could still be taken to court if a police officer thinks your driving has been affected by alcohol.

It takes about an hour for the body to get rid of the alcohol in one standard drink. So, if you have a heavy drinking session in the evening you might find that your driving ability is still affected the next morning, or you could even find that you're still over the legal limit. In addition, if you've had a few drinks at lunchtime, another one or two drinks in the early evening may well put you over the legal limit.

In a test with professional drivers, the more alcoholic drinks they had had the more certain they were that they could drive a test course through a set of moveable posts . . .and the less able they were to do it!

So the only way to be sure you're safe is not to drink at all.

Alcohol is a major cause of road traffic accidents. One in three of the drivers killed in road accidents have levels of alcohol which are over the legal limit, and road accidents after drinking are the biggest cause of death among young men. More than half of the people stopped by the police to take a breathalyzer test have a blood alcohol concentration of more than twice the legal limit.

It is important to remember that driving after you've been drinking doesn't just affect you. If you're involved in an accident it affects a lot of other people as well, not least the person you might kill or injure.

31 The amount of alcohol a person can drink before reaching the legal limit is
   A   800 mg of pure alcohol.
   B   approximately three standard drinks.
   C   different for different people.
   D   exactly proportional to body weight.

32 When might you be taken to court by the police for drinking and driving?
   A   When you have driven a vehicle after drinking any alcohol at all.
   B   When you have drunk at least three drinks before driving.
   C   Only when tests show that you have 80 mg of alcohol in 100 ml of blood.
   D   When the police think that you have been drinking from the way you are driving.

33 When you have been drinking heavily in the evening, the next day you might be
   A   still drunk until lunchtime.
   B   unable to drive until the evening.
   C   over the legal limit in the morning.
   D   unable to drive all day.

34 Alcohol is a major cause of road accidents in that
   A   most drivers who die in these accidents have been drinking.
   B   more young men die in drink-related accidents than in any other way.
   C   drinking affects people's eye-sight.
   D   one in three drivers drink heavily.

35 What does this article urge you to remember particularly about driving after drinking?
   A   You may be taken to court by the police.
   B   You are putting yourself in danger.
   C   You may hurt another road-user.
   D   You put many other people at risk.

THIRD PASSAGE

INTERNATIONAL DIRECT DIALLING

Your handy aid to International Dialling

International Direct Dialling (IDD) is the quick, easy way to telephone abroad. It is currently available to over 160 countries, and more countries are being added each year.

What you dial

Wherever you are calling you will have to dial the complete international number. In most cases this is made up of four distinct elements:

1 International Code
2 Country Code
3 Area Code
4 Customer's number

- First dial the international code. From the UK this is always 010.
- Then dial the code for the Country you require.
- Next dial the Area Code, remembering to omit any initial 0 (or 9 in the case of Finland and Spain).
- Finally dial the customer's number.

Country Codes and a brief selection of Area Codes are shown in this leaflet. Many more Area Codes are published in the International Telephone Guide (ITG). The ITG also gives hints on dialling, charging information and help with international time differences. It is available free of charge by dialling 100 and asking for Freefone 2013 (during normal working hours.)

No Area Code is required on IDD calls to some countries. Where this is the case simply dial the Customer's Number immediately after the Country Code.

Tones

After dialling you may have to wait up to one minute before hearing a tone (ringing, engaged, etc.)

Remember that tones in other countries are often different. For a free demonstration dial 100 and ask for Freefone 2070 (for Europe) or Freefone 2071 (for North America).

Should you need a code not shown or a precise time difference, or have any difficulty with the International Telephone Service, contact the international operator who will be pleased to help: the number to dial is in your Telephone Dialling Code Booklet.

PLEASE KEEP THIS LEAFLET WITH YOUR DIALLING CODE BOOKLET FOR FUTURE REFERENCE

36 What must you remember to do when dialling the Area Code?
    A To do so before dialling the Country Code.
    B To dial a nine if you are phoning Finland or France.
    C Not to dial the first number in some cases.
    D To look for it in the ITG.

37 When dialling telephone numbers abroad in some cases you can leave out
    A the third element of the code.
    B the International Code.
    C the direct dialling system.
    D the first element of the code.

38 You may have to wait for almost a minute
    A before dialling the number of the customer.
    B between dialling one code and the next.
    C after hearing a ringing tone.
    D before you hear anything.

39 Why should you dial Freefone 2013?
    A To get information about international time differences.
    B To get a list of Country Codes.
    C To get the number of the international operator.
    D To hear examples of tones.

40 What should you do if you have difficulty with an international call?
    A Dial the international code.
    B Dial one hundred, then ask for Freefone.
    C Dial International Direct Dialling.
    D Dial a number given in another booklet.

PAPER 2   COMPOSITION   (1½ hours)

*Write **two only** of the following composition exercises. Your answers must follow exactly the instructions given, and must be of between 120 and 180 words each.*

1   Write an account of a sporting or other success that you have had.

2   What are the advantages and disadvantages of people getting married and having children while they are still young?

3   A pen-friend is coming to visit you for a few weeks in July. Write a letter recommending the best way of getting to your house, the right clothes to bring, and including any other advice or requests. You should make the beginning and ending like those of an ordinary letter, but the address is not to be counted in the number of words.

4   A group from your home town is attending a conference. Write the speech you would make to introduce yourself (as group-leader) and your party.

(+ optional questions on prescribed texts)

PAPER 3   USE OF ENGLISH   (2 hours)

1   *Fill each of the numbered blanks in the following passage. Use only* **one** *word in each space.*

Our neighbours are an elderly couple, ... (1) have worked hard all

.... (2) lives. They live simply and quietly, ... (3) up early and

going to bed early every day. When the annual summer holiday arrives, they

.... (4) a week with the wife's sister, and .... (5) rest of the time

repainting and decorating their home. It is the same every year, so .... (6) of

the paintwork in the house is more than two years .... (7).

Last year, for the first time, their routine changed. For one thing, the wife's sister

was .... (8) hospital. For another, they had talked it .... (9) and

decided that for once they .... (10) take a holiday like everyone else.

They chose a caravan camp at the seaside. They .... (11) their bags,

and travelled there .... (12) train. The caravan was dirty, they said, and

people in neighbouring caravans played their radios .... (13) most of the

night. The next day was cold and wet. .... (14) they did not mind the rain,

they did mind the wind, which .... (15) the caravan shake and rock like a

boat.

That night, there was a storm. Two caravans were blown .... (16) the

sea. Their own caravan was safe, but .... (17) of them had any sleep.

.... (18) they packed their bags again, and next morning, they were at

the station, waiting for the first train home.

Now, if you ask them about holidays, they will .... (19) you: 'We don't

like holidays. We're not going .... (20) holiday again.'

2　*Finish each of the following sentences in such a way that it means exactly the same as the sentence printed before it.*

　　EXAMPLE:　I haven't enjoyed myself so much for years.

　　ANSWER:　It's years *since I enjoyed myself so much.*

a)　He borrowed my book, but he forgot to return it.

　　I ....

b)　They made him wait for two hours.

　　He was ....

c)　I must leave now, or I will miss the bus.

　　I will miss ....

d)　I can't see that far.

　　It is too ....

e)　She's a slower and more careful driver than I am.

　　She drives ....

f)　The police started looking for him two months ago.

　　For two months now the ....

g)　How old do you think this house is?

　　When do you think .... ?

h)　This holiday's so expensive, I don't think I can go.

　　It's such ....

i)   It's the cheapest watch but it's the nicest.

    Not only ....

j)   I will get home at about seven, and I'll give you a ring then.

    I'll give you a ring ....

3   *Complete the following sentences with* **one** *suitable word connected with the subject of* **time.**

    EXAMPLE: I'll see you at ten *o'clock* on Thursday morning.

a)   My watch says twenty past ten, but it is usually .... , so it's probably nearer half past.

b)   The train is due to leave at seventeen hundred .... , so we should leave here at about half past four.

c)   I found it difficult to get to sleep, and it was nearly .... before I did.

d)   Your school .... are supposed to be the happiest ones of your life.

e)   It is the low .... now, and most of the hotels are half empty.

4   *Make all the changes and additions necessary to produce, from the following sets of words and phrases, sentences which together make a complete letter. Note carefully from the example what kind of alterations need to be made. Write each sentence in the space provided.*

    EXAMPLE: Thank/letter/reach/me/Monday

    ANSWER: *Thank you for your letter, which reached me on Monday.*

    Dear John,

    Sorry/hear/car/give/trouble/again.

a)   ....

mean/not able/go/camp/July?

b) .... ?

I/tell you/when/buy it/mistake/buy/so cheap.

c) ....

After/pay/garage bills/etc./cheaper/cars/more expensive.

d) ....

My news/I/change/job/now/work/local newspaper.

e) ....

I/get/tired/old job/and/pay/not very good.

f) ....

I/in charge/car advertisement section/newspaper.

g) ....

I/try/find/better car/you?

h) .... ?

Love,

Clare

5 *Below is a plan of a house which a young family are moving into, and three suggestions on how to arrange the house. The family consists of two adults and two small girls aged five and seven.*

Using the information given, continue in about 80 words each of the two paragraphs below, giving your reasons.

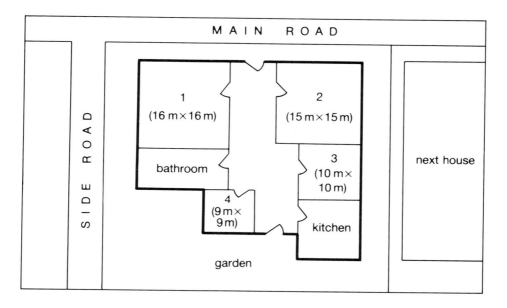

Suggestion 1:
1, sitting-room; 2, dining-room; 3, parents' bedroom; 4, children's bedroom.

Suggestion 2:
1, children's playroom; 2, living-room; 3, parents' bedroom; 4, children's bedroom.

Suggestion 3:
1, living-room; 2, parents' bedroom; 3, children's bedroom; 4, spare room, work room, playroom, etc.

The best solution would be ....

....

....

....

....

The least satisfactory solution would be ....

....

....

....

....

PAPER 4   LISTENING COMPREHENSION   (about 30 minutes)

FIRST PART

For each of questions 1–5 tick (✓) one of the boxes, A, B, C or D.

1   A photofit picture is built up by

　　A   a witness and an artist.

　　B   a policeman and a witness.

　　C   a policeman and an artist.

　　D   an artist's impression.

A
B
C
D

2   A photofit kit contains

　　A   many different pictures of faces.

　　B   515 different parts of the face.

　　C   special distinguishing marks.

　　D   pictures of different facial features.

A
B
C
D

3   Photofit works best when a witness

　　A   sees a criminal under street lights.

　　B   waits before describing the criminal.

　　C   has talked to a criminal for some time.

　　D   produces a 'type' likeness of a criminal.

A
B
C
D

4   Photofit is

　　A   not yet in colour.

　　B   drawn by computers.

　　C   used by scientists.

　　D   a big new development.

A
B
C
D

5   The Professor thinks the photofit system

　　A   has too many faults to be useful.

　　B   needs to have more British faces.

　　C   easily keeps up with new fashion.

　　D   needs more people who can use it.

A
B
C
D

SECOND PART

For question 6 number the diagrams in the order in which they are mentioned, e.g. diagram F is mentioned first so we write 1 in the box. The first diagram has been done for you.

THIRD PART

For questions 7–15 complete the missing information.

7   Number of children killed or seriously injured per year ....

8   Rear seat belts must be provided in new cars from October ....

9   Using restraints decreases risk of injury by .... %

10   Seat for child aged up to ....

11   Seat for child aged: .... to ....

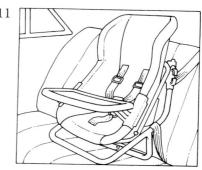

For questions 12–15 put a tick (✓) to show if the things illustrated are recommended:

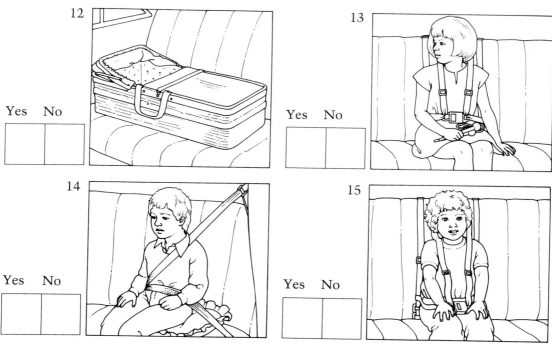

12   Yes   No

13   Yes   No

14   Yes   No

15   Yes   No

PAPER 5 INTERVIEW   (15 to 20 minutes)

SECTION A PICTURE DISCUSSION

You will be given a photograph and asked to talk about it.

Look at one of the photographs above.

a)   Describe what you can see in the photograph.
     Who do you think the men are? What are they doing?

b)   Is security a problem in your country? What do people do to protect themselves?
     What is the general attitude towards the police in your country?
     Should police be armed?

SECTION B PASSAGES FOR COMMENT

You will be given a passage to comment on.

Read one of the following passages and decide

a) whether you think it is written or spoken.
b) who is writing or speaking.
c) what the passage is about.
d) what you think about the subject.

---

1 When you cannot find the car, first think whether it may
have been removed by the police for illegal parking.
You should also be sure that you remember where you
parked it, for example, in a crowded side street or a
big car park. It is as well to make a note of where you
are leaving it as you walk away. If the car has really
gone, inform the police straight away.

---

2 A large number of criminals are caught as a result of
their own mistakes. Faced with an armed man demanding
cash, bank clerk Claudine Holder, of Temple, Texas, told
him: 'You're in the wrong line. Wait over there.' He
did as he was told, until police arrived.

---

3 Three crime-free months passed. Then I was burgled again.
The bottom of the front door had been completely broken
off. They had turned the place upside down looking for
valuables I no longer owned. They had taken the remaining
silver, a new radio-telephone, some ornaments, a leather
coat, even a half empty bottle of perfume! At least I was
insured.

SECTION C COMMUNICATION ACTIVITY

You will be asked to take part in an activity with a group of other students or your examiner.

Look at these illustrations and captions from a leaflet designed to give advice to tourists. What advice do you think the leaflet gave?

Talk about
a) the crimes which are usually committed against tourists.
b) the advice you would give to visitors to your country.

1 Protection for your car and possessions...

2 Care of valuables...

3 Don't be a hero - your life is worth more than your money...

4 In public places...

OR

Take part in a role play. You are part of a group of people on holiday abroad. In the last week a number of bombs have gone off in the town where you are staying. Nobody has been injured but the organization responsible has warned of more to come. You meet in order to decide what to do.

Take the role given to you. Prepare your role for 1 minute. Then take part in the meeting.

A	You are very worried about the situation and you want to go home but it will cost individuals a lot of money if the others do not agree. Try to persuade the others to ask the tour company to send you all home immediately.
B	You are a younger member of the group. You and your wife are enjoying your holiday and you do not want to go home. You think that foreigners and tourists will be safe and that bombs are a fact of life. Do your best to persuade the others.
C	You are a parent of two children. You are very worried about the bombs on the beaches and in hotels and you think the children will be in danger, but your partner wants to stay. Listen to the arguments and decide what to do.

PRACTICE TEST 5

PAPER 1   READING COMPREHENSION   (1 hour)

SECTION A

In this section you must choose the word or phrase which best completes each sentence.
On your answer sheet *indicate the letter, A, B, C or D, against the number of each item 1 to 25, for the word or phrase you choose.*

1   The car burst into .... but the driver managed to escape.
   A fire   B burning   C heat   D flames

2   .... ten minutes of the start of the game two players had been sent off.
   A Before   B Inside   C Around   D Within

3   It is a great .... that the exhibition was cancelled at the last minute after all your work.
   A pity   B sorrow   C complaint   D sadness

4   We have agreed .... the need for firm action.
   A on   B for   C in   D at

5   You'll have to hurry because the .... train leaves in ten minutes.
   A latter   B last   C latest   D least

6   I was pleased to see how .... she looked after her recent illness.
   A right   B pleasant   C well   D nice

7   I don't know him but he looks as if he .... be her brother.
   A can   B could   C would   D shall

8   It tasted so .... of lemon that the other flavours were lost.
   A hardly   B forcefully   C strongly   D fully

9   I think he is .... his time looking for a job there; they are not taking any staff on at present.
   A wasting   B losing   C spending   D missing

10   I don't .... to see her again until next Tuesday.
   A think   B wait   C attend   D expect

11 In the .... left-hand corner of the picture there is a white mark.
    A up   B high   C front   top

12 How old do you have to be .... you can drive a car?
    A when   B before   C until   D since

13 Let us know as soon as possible so that we can start .... arrangements.
    A having   B doing   C making   D fixing

14 The weather was warm and pleasant with .... a gentle wind to cool us down.
    A but   B just   C almost   D nearly

15 Trade Union officials and management met today to discuss the .... at the factory.
    A strike   B closing   C block   D shutting

16 I think you'd better .... before they return.
    A be gone   B being gone   C be going   D to be gone

17 A new study group has been .... by the United Nations.
    A put up   B put on   C set up   D set on

18 The hardest thing I .... to do was to look after some children for a week.
    A had never   B have ever had   C yet have   D have always had

19 This meat is rather tough; you have to .... it for a long time.
    A chew   B bite   C eat   D swallow

20 He was not very pleased about .... called an incompetent idiot.
    A being   B was   C to be   D had been

21 There is no reason to .... his honesty; he is absolutely sincere.
    A search   B doubt   C inquire   D ask

22 He has to go to Canada for the next .... of his training.
    A step   B stand   C point   D stage

23 There is bad weather at the airport, and all .... have been delayed.
    A journeys   B flights   C times   D flies

24 The interference on the radio was .... by weather conditions.
    A caused   B made   C raised   D due

25 The judge .... him twenty pounds for parking his car illegally.
    A punished   B charged   C ordered   D fined

SECTION B

In this section you will find after each of the passages a number of questions or unfinished statements about the passage, each with four suggested answers or ways of finishing. You must choose the one which you think fits best. **On your answer sheet,** *indicate the letter, A, B, C or D, against the number of each item 26 – 40 for the answer you choose. Give one answer only to each question. Read each passage right through before choosing your answers.*

FIRST PASSAGE

When I went to interview Roy Bragg yesterday I learned that new regulations, introduced in May this year, affect all forms of money-lending in Britain. This means that there have been some changes for traditional shops of the kind that Mr Bragg owns, where people can borrow money against valuable articles left at the shop until both the loan and the interest due on it are repaid. Individual money-lenders are now able to compete with each other and set their own interest rates but they have to give much more informaton to the customer at the time of the transaction.

Money-lenders now also have to apply for a licence through the government's Office of Fair Trading. The capital a money-lender requires depends on the amount he lends; if he has a lending limit of £1,000 he does not need too much. But if he intends to lend large amounts, says Roy Bragg, who once lent £45,000 on some rare books, 'he should watch out he doesn't get as short of money as his customers. My money is in and out every day of the week.'

He and his staff are all Fellows of the Gemological Association. It is an essential qualification for valuing jewellery, though they also learn by experience whether items are genuine or not. 'When I first started, I never knew it would be so difficult,' said one of Roy Bragg's young assistants. 'On my own, I wouldn't have got anywhere; I would have offered too much or too little.'

Roy Bragg agrees that you can never accept anything or anybody unquestioningly in the money-lending business. 'Some of the best-dressed and most well-spoken people are the ones you have to watch. One of the oldest tricks is for someone to come in and show you a large, real diamond ring. You say they can have £1,000 on it. They say, "Oh no, I wanted £1,500. I'll go somewhere else." You pass the ring back and they don't go away, just take it from you and turn towards the door. Then they turn back and say, "Oh, I don't know, I was recommended to you. I think I'll take the £1,000." And meanwhile they've done a switch with a cheaper ring. I tell my staff that if an item leaves their hands they should inspect it again as if it had just arrived.'

How do they know they are not dealing in stolen property? 'After forty-four years, you get a nose for this kind of thing,' says Roy Bragg. 'Most of us in the trade know each other well. I'm on the Committee of the National Association: we meet once a month and know if anyone's having any bother.'

26 What difference have the new regulations made to the money-lending business?
    A Interest rates are much more variable.
    B Money-lenders cannot operate without a licence.
    C More information has to be given to the government.
    D Customers now ask more questions.

27 What we learn from Roy Bragg about the amount of capital money-lenders need?
    A £45,000 is about the right amount.
    B They must balance their lending policy and their capital.
    C They will need more than they first thought.
    D The Office of Fair Trading sets limits.

28 What did Mr Bragg's young assistant find was tending to happen when he first began to work for the business?
    A He misjudged what customers wanted.
    B He damaged precious articles.
    C He over-valued everything.
    D He needed help from more experienced staff.

29 Money-lenders have to be suspicious about
    A everyone who comes to them.
    B people who look poor.
    C people who look rich.
    D anybody who brings valuable items.

30 In the old trick described a money-lender might make the mistake of
    A not recognizing stolen property.
    B offering £500 too much.
    C not realizing there were two rings.
    D not examining the ring carefully in the first place.

31 How does Mr Bragg know when he is being offered things which have been stolen?
    A He gets information from the police.
    B Experience tells him when something is wrong.
    C He can now recognize all the local burglars.
    D The National Association sends out warnings.

SECOND PASSAGE

New roof for an old cottage

In this world of new technology it is good to know that some of the old skills and crafts are still practised. One such traditional craft is thatching—making roofs from straw or reeds—and one of the few remaining thatched cottages in the Wellington area, Linden Cottage at Westford, has just been given an attractive new roof.

Walkers using the footway past the cottage will no doubt have noticed the new roof, which also covers an area over the front door, and the owner, Mr Dennis Wright and his wife, Pam, say they are delighted with the end result. 'It's an old craft which cannot be rushed,' said Mrs Wright. 'The cottage now looks better than ever.'

The work, which took about six weeks, was carried out by Brian Whitemore and Robert Webber of Lydeard Saint Lawrence. Until now the 300-year-old cottage was roofed with wheat straw which lasts on average for fifteen years but this time Mr and Mrs Wright decided to have the roof done with water reeds which last for sixty or seventy years and cost more.

Signs that re-roofing is needed are when straw washes out in heavy rain and the fixings begin to show. The water reeds, which are brought from Scotland, are thicker and longer than wheat straw but are slightly more difficult for the craftsmen to use. Water reeds also differ from wheat straw in that iron hooks are used to keep them in place, whereas with the old straw roof, wooden pegs were used.

After the wheat straw was taken off, the worn wood in the roof was renewed and the cross-pieces which lie over the roof beams were also replaced. Large waterproof sheets were erected to keep everything dry. Although Linden Cottage will not have to be completely re-roofed for many years, like all thatched properties it will still have to be 'ridged' after every eight years. This means that the join at the top of the house is redone to maintain its strength.

The cottage has been re-roofed twice in the thirty-one years that Mr and Mrs Wright have lived there—the last time was in 1969. As it has now been officially declared a building of special historic interest which must be preserved, the ridging can only be done in the West Country style, and other patterns of ridging are not acceptable. The roof is now bright yellow in colour but it will quickly become darker as it weathers.

Brian Whitemore has been in the roofing business for about thirty years and he and his partner cover a wide area. Working with them at Linden Cottage were brothers Lee and Steven Roadhouse from Bishops Lydeard who are training to become thatchers. While they were there Brian's small dog, Midge, became a star attraction as he ran up and down their ladder while they worked. He travels almost everywhere with them and is as much part of the scenery as the ladder.

32 Mr and Mrs Wright, the owners of Linden Cottage,
    A   have spent a long time looking for someone to do the roof.
    B   are surprised at how difficult it was to do the roof.
    C   were very pleased at how well the work was done.
    D   found they had to choose cheaper roofing material.

33 The new thatched roof at Linden Cottage will last for approximately
    A   eight years.
    B   fifteen years.
    C   seventy years.
    D   three hundred years.

34 What was different about how the roof was done this time compared with the previous time?
    A   A cloth lining was installed.
    B   New wooden pegs were made.
    C   Iron hooks were used to hold the thatch.
    D   The wooden frame to the roof was re-designed.

35 Because Linden Cottage has now been declared of special historic interest the roof
    A   has to be finished in a certain way.
    B   has to be thatched with water reeds.
    C   must be yellow in colour.
    D   has to be redone more frequently.

36 How many people worked on the new roofing?
    A   One.
    B   Two.
    C   Four.
    D   Five.

THIRD PASSAGE

HOW TO ORDER

Ladies' wear

When ordering dresses, coats, skirts and knitwear, do so by size number only. Ask a friend to help you take your bust, waist and hip measurements, then obtain your size number from the chart.

A	Measure around fullest part of bust, keeping tape level.
B	Measure around natural waistline.
C	Measure around fullest part of hips (about 20 cm below waist) keeping tape level.

Length of garments

D	Measure skirt from natural waist to hem.
E	Measure coats from centre back to the length required.
F	Measure dresses from centre back shoulder to length required.

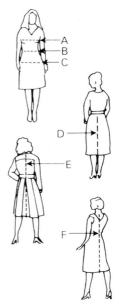

Men's wear

When ordering suits, trousers and jeans, you need to know your size number and fitting. These are shown in the chart with a number and a letter. The number indicates the chest or waist measurement. The letter indicates the fitting.

A	Measure chest over shirt, well up under arms and over shoulder blades, keeping the tape level.
B	Measure the natural waistline (NOT over trousers), keeping tape level.
C	Measure jackets or coats from top of centre (where the collar joins the back) to the length required.

Measuring trousers and jeans

Inside leg measurement. The easiest, most accurate way to ensure the correct length is to take a pair of trousers which you consider a good fit, lay them on a flat surface and measure down the inside leg seam. Remember to take into account the shoes or boots to be worn with the item you are ordering.

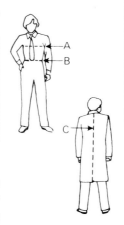

You have a Mail Order clothing catalogue and have been asked to order some items for friends and relatives.

37   To order a woman's dress you will need to give
   A   one number.
   B   two numbers.
   C   three numbers.
   D   six numbers.

38   To order a man's suit you will need to give
   A   a number.
   B   a number and a letter.
   C   chest and waist measurements.
   D   chest, waist and length measurements.

39   How does taking measurements when ordering men's clothing differ from taking measurements when ordering women's clothing?
   A   You don't have to take as many measurements.
   B   You can measure on top of normal clothing.
   C   You don't need to measure lengths.
   D   You have to measure for a closer fit.

40   To get the correct leg length when ordering any trousers you should
   A   measure from waist to boots or shoes.
   B   remove boots or shoes before measuring.
   C   lie down flat before measuring.
   D   measure another pair of trousers.

PAPER 2   COMPOSITION   (1½ hours)

*Write **two only** of the following composition exercises. Your answers must follow exactly the instructions given, and must be of between 120 and 180 words each.*

1   Write a letter to complain about a journey that went wrong. You should make the beginning and ending like those of an ordinary letter, but the address is not to be counted in the number of words.

2   You are going to show some visitors around your home area. Write the speech you would make to them explaining what they are going to do and see.

3   Write an account of an important recent day in your life.

4   Write a description of a person who has influenced your life or thoughts.

(+ optional questions on prescribed texts)

PAPER 3   USE OF ENGLISH   (2 hours)

1   *Fill each of the numbered blanks in the following passage. Use only **one** word in each space.*

In that part of the world, it was snobbish to own an English car. My contact there, a successful businessman, had decided to prove his success by getting, not

.... (1) an English car, a vastly expensive antique Rolls Royce,

.... (2) also a right-hand drive one. The car had .... (3) to be

shipped specially from England. The instructions were in English, with the instruments

in miles rather .... (4) kilometres, and degrees Fahrenheit ....

(5) of degrees Centigrade. My friend was immensely proud .... (6) it. A real,

English Rolls Royce, he said, was the .... (7) of fashion. His friends, he said,

would be green .... (8) envy.

   The car arrived, and two days .... (9) we had to make a trip to a town

three hours .... (10) away. We set off in the hot morning sun, getting

admiring .... (11) from people in the street. My friend spoke

enthusiastically of his car. It was .... (12) a pleasure to drive, he said, that

he .... (13) not imagine why everyone .... (14) not buy one.

   Out .... (15) the open road, we went faster. The air was hot now, and

my friend tried to switch on the air-conditioning. .... (16) he could find was

a heater. I told him that, in England, heaters were more necessary than air-conditioning.

He would not .... (17) me. He tried all the other switches, but kept

returning to the heater. The outside air, which was already uncomfortably hot and dry,

was made .... (18) hotter, and was blown into the car. Again and again, he

tried the switches. Again and again a blast of hot air hit us. It was painful to breathe. 'I'm

sending this car .... (19) back to the makers,' he gasped. 'There's

.... (20) badly wrong with the air-conditioning.'   99

2   *Finish each of the following sentences in such a way that it means exactly the same as the sentence printed before it.*

EXAMPLE: I haven't enjoyed myself so much for years.

ANSWER: It's years *since I enjoyed myself so much.*

a)   We had never been so happy before.

We were   ....

b)   I'm sorry that I didn't learn to ride a bicycle when I was younger.

I regret   ....

c)   The police made the boat turn back.

The boat   ....

d)   I have never been to the ballet before.

It's   ....

e)   He spoke so quickly that I couldn't understand what he said.

He spoke too   ....

f)   She asked John to repeat what he had said.

'Please   ....

g)   She didn't work hard enough, so she lost her job.

The reason   ....

h)   I'm grateful that you looked after my mother so well.

Thank you   ....

i)   It's impossible to cross the road because of the traffic.

The traffic makes it   ....

j)   The switch was too high for him to reach.

He wasn't tall ....

3   *Complete the following sentences with* **one** *appropriate word connected with the subjects of* **food** *and* **eating.**

EXAMPLE: We usually have our main *meal* in the evening.

a)   This is a typical Italian .... made of meat and pasta.

b)   It was a proper dinner, with three .... followed by fruit and cheese.

c)   She liked the dessert so much, she asked him to write down the .... for it, so she could try to make it herself.

d)   He's not allowed to eat bread or potatoes, because the doctor has told him to go on a .... and lose some weight.

e)   I don't know exactly what is in this, but there is a strong .... of cheese.

4   *Make all the changes and additions necessary to produce, from the following sets of words and phrases, sentences which will complete the conversation. Note carefully from the example what kinds of alterations need to be made. Write each sentence in the space provided.*

EXAMPLE: Peter: I/decide/look/for/somewhere/else/live.

ANSWER: *I've decided to look for somewhere else to live.*

Susan: I thought you liked it where you live.

Peter: become/so expensive/not/afford/live/there.

a)   ....

Susan: I know. Anywhere round here is expensive now.

Peter: How much/last/electricity bill?

b)   ....

Susan: I can't remember. We pay all our bills together.

Peter: last bill/come to/over £200.

c)   ....

Susan: Yes, that is a lot. How did that happen?

Peter: flat/very cold/spend/lot/heating.

d)   ....

Susan: Anyway, it's not easy to find flats round here, is it?

Peter: look/new flat/three weeks/now/can't/find.

e)   ....

Susan: Well, I'll let you know if I hear of anything.

Peter: mention/your friends/office?

f)   ....

Susan: Yes, certainly, I'll ask them.

Peter: waste/time/look/newspapers.

g)   ....

Susan: Why, are the flats all too expensive?

Peter: good/always/go/by the time/telephone.

h)   ....

5   *You are planning a trip to a Greek island for two weeks' holiday, and are deciding how to travel there. You have a party of eight people, including three adults, three teenagers and two young children. Below is a table giving information about the different ways of getting there.*

Using the information given, continue in about 60 words each of the paragraphs started for you below, giving your reasons.

	Scheduled flight	Charter flight	Coach/ boat	Train/ boat
Length of journey	2 hours	2 hours	14 hours	12 hours
Cost per adult	£460	£140	£80	£120
Children's fare	90%	70%	50%	50%
Frequency	4 flights per day	1 flight per week	1 departure per day	4 departures per day
Baggage limit	20 kg per adult	20 kg per adult	40 kg per adult	no limit

I would suggest as first choice   ....

....

....

....

....

I would suggest as second choice ....

....

....

....

....

I would not suggest ....

....

....

....

....

PAPER 4 LISTENING COMPREHENSION (about 30 minutes)

FIRST PART

For questions 1–7 tick (✓) the box to show whether you think the statement is true or false.

	True	False
1 The main subject of the talk is how to prevent crimes from happening to you.		
2 More burglaries happen at night than in the daytime.		
3 In London last year there were three burglaries a minute.		
4 The majority of burglars are not professionals.		
5 You should follow the example of the 86 year-old woman.		
6 When there are burglars in the house you should scream to make them panic.		
7 Don't go into a house if you think someone has broken in.		

For questions 8 – 9 complete these notes on the talk. Be as brief as possible.

8   If you hear a burglar in the house at night, lock the bedroom door before you

a) ....

OR

b) ....

9   If your attacker has a weapon you should keep calm and

a) follow ....

b) give him time to ....

SECOND PART

For questions 10–17 complete the information on this form.

BENNET'S GARAGE LTD

Car registration number (10) ....

Service (11) .... miles

Special instructions:

(12) _____   _____ door

(13) _____ light

Date in: (14) ....

Courtesy car required?   (15) Yes ☐ No ☐

Headlights adjusted?   (16) Yes ☐ No ☐

Car required by (17) ....

THIRD PART

For question 18 you will hear an expert giving a listener advice about moving house. Tick the advice you hear the expert give. The first one has been done for you.

Advice given

a)	Hire a large van.	
b)	Use a removal firm.	✓
c)	Get more than one estimate.	
d)	Move at weekends.	
e)	Send your children away.	
f)	Pack little boxes yourself.	
g)	Read your meter before you move.	
h)	Arrange to connect your washing machine.	
i)	If packing yourself, collect containers in supermarkets.	
j)	Don't pack all your books in one box.	
k)	Protect fragile things.	
l)	Pack everything you need.	
m)	Label all your boxes.	
n)	Clean up before you go.	

PAPER 5   INTERVIEW   (15 to 20 minutes)

N.B. In this test we have deliberately not given any suggested questions for sections A and B, in order to give students experience of conditions in the examination itself.

SECTION A   PICTURE DISCUSSION

Talk about one of the photographs below.

SECTION B PASSAGES FOR COMMENT

Comment on one of the following passages.

1 Accidents have increased by 29%, which is well above the
   growth in the volume of traffic, and a frightening 45%
   of all accidents involve cyclists. This is nearly three
   times the national urban average. Last year, five
   cyclists were killed, 161 had serious injuries and 534
   had minor injuries. The report comes to the conclusion
   that the cyclist was to blame in almost half of these
   cases.

2 The most important development in transport is the social
   consequences of the motor vehicle and particularly the
   car. Some people say it is the most anti-social device
   ever offered to the public; others, like myself, see it
   as a mixed blessing, one which has given us a lot of
   trouble but has nevertheless given pleasure to millions
   of people in the world beyond anything they could ever
   have dreamt of fifty years ago.

3 I've just moved to London and I'm a lot happier. It was
   soul-destroying spending hours on the train every day.
   I was never home before dark...and all that time spent
   travelling...it would be all right if the trains were
   pleasant but they're always crowded and it's not easy
   trying to read or do some work when someone's sitting
   on top of you. I'm glad that's behind me.

SECTION C   COMMUNICATION ACTIVITY

Take part in one of the following activities.

Look at these illustrations from a guide for drivers and cyclists.
Why do you think this guide was produced?

HOW CYCLISTS SHOULD BEHAVE

The rules that apply to other road users apply to you as well, such as at traffic lights, pedestrian crossings and one-way streets. Riding with little regard for others causes anger, frustration and accidents!

Look behind before changing direction and signal in good time.

How many times have you heard motorists saying "Sorry, I didn't see him"? Make sure you can be seen by others both day and night.

A bike is very mobile in traffic but sudden swerves and zig-zagging cannot be anticipated by motorists.

Remember that two-thirds of all cycle accidents happen at roundabouts and junctions. Get eye to eye contact with drivers – have they seen you? **Ride defensively.**

Plan your route – use cycle tracks and routes when they're available.

MAKE SURE YOU CAN BE SEEN BY OTHERS BOTH DAY AND NIGHT

HOW MOTORISTS CAN HELP

Cyclists are particularly vulnerable at roundabouts and junctions. Remember that bikes amount to only one quarter of the frontal area of a car – they're easy to miss, particularly when you're concentrating on other traffic.

Watch out for cyclists

– **when turning right into side roads** ▶

◀ – **when turning out of side streets into main roads**

– **when turning left into side streets** ▶

ANTICIPATE THE ACTIONS OF CYCLISTS

Do many people use bicycles or motorcycles in your country?
Do you think they are dangerous? Why/Why not?
Discuss these questions so that you agree on the advice you would give to
a)   a young person who is riding a bicycle for the first time.
b)   drivers so that they can reduce the number of accidents involving cyclists.

OR

Use these diagrams from an accident report to work out the details of the accident.

You were one of the people involved in the accident. Describe how the accident happened from your point of view.

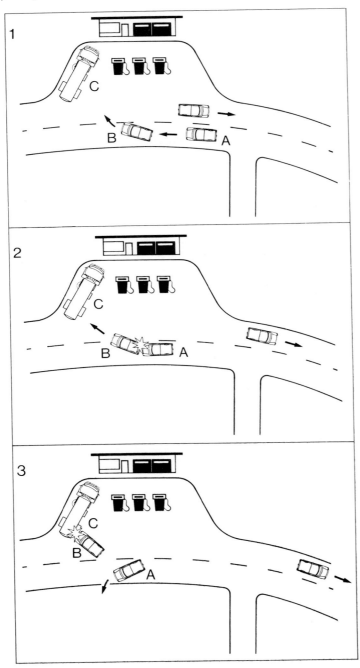

Key

PRACTICE TEST I

PAPER 1   READING COMPREHENSION   (1 hour)

SECTION A   1 mark for each correct answer

1 C	6 D	11 A	16 C	21 C
2 B	7 A	12 C	17 D	22 D
3 B	8 A	13 D	18 C	23 B
4 C	9 D	14 B	19 C	24 B
5 D	10 C	15 C	20 A	25 A

SECTION B   2 marks for each correct answer

26 A	31 C	36 B
27 D	32 D	37 C
28 B	33 A	34 B
29 C	34 B	39 D
30 B	35 D	40 A

Total = 55 marks   Pass = about 33 marks

PAPER 2   COMPOSITION   (1½ hours)

See Introduction for marking criteria.

Total = 40 marks   Pass = about 16 marks

PAPER 3   USE OF ENGLISH   (2 hours)

1   1 mark for each correct answer

1	in/near	9	to	16	very/quite/
2	had	10	very/totally/completely/		obviously/clearly
3	one		really etc.	17	by
4	at/for	11	least	18	clear/definite
5	what	12	on	19	led
6	whether	13	were	20	else/different
7	else	14	as		
8	by	15	at/round/over		Total = 20 marks

2   Give marks as shown for sections in italics

a   It was *so hot* (that) I nearly fainted.   2
b   I'm really looking *forward to going* to the theatre tomorrow.   2
c   It's the first time *I've (ever) eaten* this.   2
d   I wonder *if/whether it's possible* to travel to London by coach.   1
e   I wish *you had told us* about this.   2
f   He's *having the/his windows* mended (by someone).   2
g   It *has been raining since* two o'clock.   2
h   She was *made to hand* over her passport.   2
i   It's not *as good as* I thought (it would be).   2
j   It was *such a sweet cake* that I *couldn't eat it*.   3

Total = 20 marks

3   1 mark for each correct answer

a   unexpectedly
b   informative
c   action
d   lengthens
e   suitable

Total = 5 marks

4   Give marks as shown for sections in italics

a   *I have written to you* three times *in/during* the last two months.   3
b   *I have also tried telephoning/to telephone* (you) several times.   2
c   Each time *I have found it* impossible *to get through to you*.   3
d   *I am afraid* (that) *I find your* attitude unacceptable.   3
e   I now feel this *has gone on* long enough.   2
f   *It is now time to find a solution to* the problem/*that a solution to* the problem was found.   2
g   I *have therefore decided to write* this last letter.   2
h   *If there is/I have (had) no reply by/before* the end of this week *you will hear/will be hearing* from my lawyers.   3

Total = 20 marks

5   In this question the student should be able to choose relevant material, and then present the facts in a reasonably fluent form.

Any choice may be made but good reasons should be offered for the choice.

The answer should contain carefully chosen information, written in a continuous style, but should not be too long.

5 marks for each paragraph taking into account the above points.

The following notes suggest some possible reasons:

My first choice would be . . . children's camp: plenty to do; educational as well as leisure activities; no worries about supervision of children since camp's trained staff deal with this and plan the activities.

My second choice would be . . . mountaineering/horse-riding: variety of scenery; new experiences if from city; good exercise; other things to study, animal care, geography etc.; adventure under supervision.

I would not recommend . . . major historical cities: too much travel; not enough variety; too large a group? limited interest.

Total = 15 marks

Final total = 80 marks   Pass = about 40 marks

PAPER 4   LISTENING COMPREHENSION   (about 30 minutes)

FIRST PART   1 mark for each correct answer

1	8,000	6	170
2	to feed	7	A photograph
3	£30	8	Your name
4	50	9	WD1 4RY
5	£1,500	10	0231 – 722519

Total = 10 marks

SECOND PART   ½ mark for each correct answer

11	F	16	T
12	F	17	F
13	T	18	T
14	F	19	T
15	T	20	F

Total = 5 marks

THIRD PART   1 mark for each correct answer

21	B	24	D
22	D	25	C
23	C		

Total = 5 marks

Final total = 20 marks

Tapescript

FIRST PART

For the first part of the test you will hear an interview with the director of a zoo. He is talking about a new idea at the zoo. Look at questions 1 to 10. Complete the advertisement by filling in the appropriate spaces. You will hear the piece twice.

Pause

Tone

Presenter 1:	And now Sue Lawson with news of a new idea at Woodbridge Zoo. Sue . . .
Sue Lawson:	Are you an animal lover? Well, if you are, your visits to Woodbridge Zoo can be even more exciting and worthwhile because this is the chance not only to see one of the largest collections of animals in the world, but to visit your very own animal. And this is because every animal (and there are more than 8,000 at Woodbridge Zoo), is waiting to be adopted by you or your family, by a group like a school class or even by a company. I have with me David Jones, the Zoo's Director. David, who is the Adopt An Animal scheme open to?
David Jones:	Well, it's open to any individual or any group with an interest in saving the world's wildlife from further depletion.
Sue Lawson:	Why should we think about adopting an animal?
David Jones:	Erm, well as you know Woodbridge Zoo is one of the most famous zoos in the world, and along with Winterton Park it forms our National Zoological Collection. Many of its animals are now endangered species which could well disappear if we don't look after them. Now they're very difficult to keep and breed and expensive to feed and because we're a registered charity we rely on the public for donations and help and so what better way to help those animals and make your visits more enjoyable than to adopt an animal? What's more, an adoption would make a very special present for someone . . .
Sue Lawson:	How does the scheme work?
David Jones:	The scheme is based on what it costs to keep and feed an animal for one year. These costs are broken down into adoption units of £30. For example, it costs just about £30 to keep a snake like a boa-constrictor, so if you were to buy one £30 adoption unit you could adopt a boa-constrictor for a whole year. On the other hand a lion costs around £1,500, (fifteen hundred pounds), so, for £30 you could buy one of the 50 units available for each lion in the Zoo. Naturally, you can buy as many units as you want so if you'd like to buy all 170 units and adopt an elephant, we'd be delighted, and so would the elephant. But it can cost less. Some of the very small animals only cost about £10 a year to feed so . . . so many of the tiny birds and mammals, reptiles, insects as well as some of the fish can be adopted for only £10.
Sue Lawson:	But do you get anything for your money?
David Jones:	Oh yes! If you decide to buy a £30 unit you'll get an adoption certificate, a photograph of the animal you've adopted, a complimentary ticket for free entrance (or a group season ticket if you're group adopters) and your name on a special sign near the animal's enclosure. You'll also get copies of our newsletter. For £10 you get the same but without the photograph.

Sue Lawson: So how would any of our listeners become an adopter?
David Jones: It really is very easy. If they write or telephone:
              Adopt An Animal
              Woodbridge Zoo
              Queen's Park
              Woodbridge WD1 4RY
              Telephone 0231–722519, that's 0231–722519,
              we'll send them an application form and a list of animals that are still
              available for adoption.
Sue Lawson: Thank you, David. And we'll be giving you that address again at the end of the
              programme . . .

Pause

Now you will hear the piece again. Rewind the tape and listen.

That is the end of the first part of the test.

SECOND PART

In the second part of the test you will hear part of a radio programme about a boy with a rare medical problem. Look at questions 11 to 20. For each of the questions tick one box to show whether the statement is true or false. You will hear the piece twice.

Pause
Tone

Male voice: Tonight, in 'Strange but True' we look at the case of Jason, a boy in a hundred
              million who's never had a meal in his life. Sue Roberts reports.
Sue: Each evening when the White family sit down for their evening meal their
              son Jason is missing. He's busy watching television or playing with his
              computer because, strange though it may sound, this active 14-year-old boy
              can't eat.
              Jason was born with a rare digestive fault called vasoactive intestinal
              polypeptide syndrome (or VIP). There are only forty known cases in the world.
              Doctors think there is a tumour or growth that prevents him from digesting
              food. If they found the tumour he would be cured, but until they do, he takes
              in his 3,000 calories of food each day in the form of three litres of liquid. He
              does quite well on his diet (Jason is 1.57 metres tall and weighs 57 kilos) but
              since he had his stomach removed by doctors when he was a two-year-old in
              order to try to remove the tumour, he has not been able to take normal food.
              He has an artificial stomach and his mother says that he doesn't really miss
              food. As he's never eaten anything he doesn't know what he's missing. Jason
              has to carry drip bags containing his liquid diet with him all the time. The
              bags are hung from his shoulders and a small portable pump which he wears

117

at his side makes sure he gets the right amount of liquid food. Because of all this, strangers sometimes call him 'spaceman'. Jason lives with his family in a town called Hope, in the USA. He cannot go to school because it's very easy for him to pick up infections and so he's taught at home. The cost of survival has been very high and his medical treatment has already cost more than $500,000. That money was provided by medical insurance but it's now run out and the family are having to spend their life savings on Jason. Everyone is looking forward to the day when Jason can enjoy a hamburger like so many other children of his age.

Pause

Now you will hear the piece again. Rewind the tape and listen.

That is the end of the second part of the test.

THIRD PART

In the third part of the test you will hear part of a phone-in programme on the radio. Look at questions 21 to 25. For questions 21 to 25 tick one of the boxes A, B, C or D to show the correct answer. You will hear the piece twice.

Pause
Tone

Jim:	Our guest today is Duncan White who is President of the Association of Travel Agents. During the programme we'll talk to him about the Association, his role in it, and most importantly what it can do for you but our first caller, Mrs Hopkins of Manchester, is on the line. Mrs Hopkins . . .
Mrs Hopkins:	Hello Jim. Nice to talk to you. Thank you for giving me a chance to appear on your show.
Jim:	That's all right my dear, how can we help you? What's your problem?
Mrs Hopkins:	Well, my husband and I booked this holiday in Corfu through a local travel agent. That was in May. Now, what we wanted was a quiet little hotel near the beach for the kids, you see we've got two little ones aged three and four and so this travel agent recommended the Hotel Solara which looked just like what we wanted in the brochure . . .
Jim:	And what was the Hotel Solara like?
Mrs Hopkins:	Well, that's just it! We never stayed there. When we arrived at the airport we were met by the tour representative who was very nice and apologetic but she said she was taking us to another hotel 'cos the Solara was booked up. Well, you know how it is with two kids on a night flight so we just went along with it but in the morning when we had a chance to look around, it just wasn't what we wanted.

Jim: Why was that?

Mrs Hopkins: Well, the hotel was more expensive, and very modern and all that but it was one of those really big hotels with hundreds of tourists and not a bit personal. Just like a factory really, and it was miles from the beach, well at least it was a lot further than the Solara and it was very noisy at night. These groups'd come back from the bar singing, the kids'd wake up, not a hotel for a family at all. Anyway, we complained several times but they wouldn't move us, so we ended up coming home early and we even had to pay extra for the flight. It was really disappointing and I think we ought to get our money back . . .

Jim: Well, Duncan, what do you think?

Duncan: Yes, Mrs Hopkins, a most unfortunate experience and I'm sorry to hear that your holiday was spoiled. Can I ask you a few more details? Firstly, is your travel agent a member of the Association of Travel Agents?

Mrs Hopkins: Oh, I don't know, they're quite a big firm in Manchester . . .

Duncan: Sounds as though they might be. Now, have you been back to them?

Mrs Hopkins: Well, no, 'cos we complained to the representative in Corfu and that didn't seem to get us anywhere and we didn't see the point . . .

Duncan: Right, first find out if your travel agent is a member of our Association. You see, all our members have promised to do all they can to avoid overbooking but they can't guarantee that some hotels will not be overbooked by the hotel management. If overbooking is discovered before you leave they must offer you another holiday which is at least as good, if there is one, or your money back immediately. If however overbooking is discovered after you leave, tour operators must find you somewhere else to stay. They must also return some of your money if the hotel facilities and location are of a lower standard than booked. Now, in your case it seems that the hotel you were sent to was of a higher standard although it wasn't what you wanted. I think you should go to the travel agent you bought the holiday from and talk it through with him. You may find him very sympathetic. If your complaint is not settled, and your agent is one of our members, our Association would be willing to look into it if you sent us full details. We'll give you the address later. Unfortunately, if the tour operator is not one of us you're unlikely to get anything . . . but go and have a word with the agent first.

Jim: Thanks for calling, Mrs Hopkins.

Mrs Hopkins: Thank *you* Jim, I'll try that . . .

Pause

Now you will hear the piece again. Rewind the tape and listen.

That is the end of the third part of the test. There will now be a pause to allow you to check your work.

Pause

Tone

That is the end of the test.

PAPER 5   INTERVIEW   (15 to 20 minutes)

SECTION B   PASSAGES FOR COMMENT

Suggested answers:

1   a) Could be spoken or written (perhaps to a problem page in a magazine?)
    b) The mother of a 15-year-old boy
    c) She is worried that her son might be stealing things from his class-mates at school.

2   a) Probably spoken
    b) A teenager who is just about to/has just left school
    c) He or she doesn't want to go to university and would rather travel.

3   a) Probably spoken
    b) Someone giving advice to a mother of a teenage son
    c) The son has dyed his hair and likes punks, and the mother is worried.

See Introduction for marking criteria for Interview paper.

Total = 30 marks   Pass = about 18 marks

PRACTICE TEST 2

PAPER 1   READING COMPREHENSION   (1 hour)

SECTION A   1 mark for each correct answer

1 D	6 B	11 B	16 B	21 D
2 A	7 D	12 C	17 A	22 C
3 B	8 B	13 C	18 D	23 D
4 A	9 D	14 C	19 C	24 C
5 C	10 B	15 B	20 B	25 B

SECTION B   2 marks for each correct answer

26 B	31 B	36 C
27 C	32 D	37 D
28 D	33 D	38 C
29 A	34 B	39 B
30 B	35 B	40 D

Total = 55 marks   Pass = about 33 marks

PAPER 2   COMPOSITION   (1½ hours)

See Introduction for marking criteria.

Total = 40 marks   Pass = about 16 marks

PAPER 3   USE OF ENGLISH   (2 hours)

1   1 mark for each correct answer

1	on/about	12	see/read
2	more	13	without
3	got/arrived/reached	14	so
4	later	15	end
5	on	16	more
6	contain/be	17	reached
7	would	18	with/in
8	from	19	so
9	out	20	another
10	hand		
11	hearing		Total = 20 marks

2   Give marks as shown for sections in italics

    a   It was *such bad weather* (that) we couldn't go out.   2
    b   We *have been writing* to each other *for six years*.   2
    c   I went to that school and *so did my brother*.   2
    d   That's the last time *I'm ever going to visit* them/*I'll ever visit* them/*I ever visit them*.   2
    e   Neither she *nor I had ever been* there before.   2
    f   That question *has never been discussed* (by anyone).   2
    g   He *must/has to be met* at the railway station (by someone).   2
    h   She *told him/her etc. not to be* late.   2
    i   I am used *to getting up* early.   2
    j   He was so far away *(that) he didn't/couldn't hear* me.   2

Total = 20 marks

3   1 mark for each correct answer

    a   department/dept.
    b   check-out/till/cash desk
    c   tool/hardware
    d   fit
    e   sale(s)

Total = 5 marks

4   Give marks as shown for sections in italics

    a   When *are you leaving?*/When *will you leave?*   2
    b   *Are you going by* train or (by) car?/*Will you go by* train or (by) car?   2
    c   *Do you mind if I use/my using* the car on Saturday morning?   3
    d   When *have I ever crashed?* (When *did I ever crash?*)   2
    e   What *makes you think I'll crash/I'm going to crash?*   3
    f   *Don't you trust me?*   3
    g   Where *will you leave* the car keys?   2
    h   *Won't/Don't you need* the car on Friday?   2

Total = 19 marks

SECTION B

5   In this question the student should be able to choose relevant material and then present the facts in a reasonably fluent form.

Any choice may be made but good reasons should be offered for the choice.

The answer should contain carefully chosen information written in a continuous style, but should not be too long.

Give 4 marks for each paragraph taking into account the above points.

The following are notes for a suggested answer:

Nice to have a sports club but these facilities only for people who like sport. Free one day a week, when it might become very crowded.

Good to have shopping area with plenty of parking especially if there are also local shops. Perhaps could have indoor fountain and attractive area by the restaurant.

Heavily populated/industrial area. Advantage to have 'green belt' and open space. But not much money in this.

Best is Acme plan, because would appeal to majority of people.

Total = 16 marks

Final total = 80 marks   Pass = about 40 marks

PAPER 4   LISTENING COMPREHENSION   (about 30 minutes)

FIRST PART   Give marks as shown

1	100	½ mark		8	30	½ mark
2	1 egg	1 mark		9	220	½ mark
3	milk	½ mark		10	25	½ mark
4	melted butter	1 mark		11	a noise	½ mark
5	lumps	½ mark		12	30 minutes	½ mark
6	egg	½ mark		13	brown	½ mark
7	butter	½ mark				

Total = 7½ marks

SECOND PART   Give marks as shown

14	1300	½ mark		19	Sheffield	1 mark
15	1856	½ mark		20	(92.5%) pure/of good quality	1 mark
16	1423	½ mark				
17	B	½ mark		21	the maker	1 mark
18	D	½ mark		22	the date (it was made)	1 mark

Total = 6½ marks

THIRD PART   Give marks as shown

23	Anna Leung	1 mark		28	F	½ mark
24	Captain's Bar	½ mark		29	F	½ mark
25	7.30 pm	½ mark		30	T	½ mark
26	8.30 pm	½ mark		31	F	½ mark
27	2.10 pm	½ mark		32	F	½ mark
				33	T	½ mark

Total = 6 marks

Final total = 20 marks

Tapescript

FIRST PART

For the first part of the test you will hear a woman telling you how to make Yorkshire Pudding. Look at questions 1 to 13. Complete the notes by filling in the spaces provided. You will hear the piece twice.

Pause
Tone

Katie Foyle: Hello! Today, I'd like to tell you how to make that most traditional of English dishes – Yorkshire Pudding. Today Yorkshire Pudding is usually served with roast beef but it was originally introduced as a way of filling you up before you got to your main meal of meat and vegetables. In order to make a traditional Yorkshire Pudding you need to start by making a batter which is essentially a mixture of flour and milk. For this you need:
　　100 grams of flour
　　1 egg
　　salt
　　250 millilitres of milk
　　and 1 tablespoon of melted butter
Start by putting the flour and a small teaspoon of salt into a bowl. Make sure that there are no lumps in the flour. Add the egg, the melted butter and half the milk and beat the mixture until it's like thick cream. You can then add the rest of the milk. Leave the mixture to stand until the meat is about half an hour from being cooked.
The secret of Yorkshire Pudding is a hot oven, so make sure the oven is at 220 degrees centigrade or gas mark 7. Put butter, or the fat which has dripped off the beef, into a 25 centimetre by 30 centimetre baking-tin and heat it in the oven until the tin begins to smoke gently. Pour the batter in. It should make a noise as it goes in. Bake the mixture in the centre of the oven for about 30 minutes. You should then reduce the temperature to 200 degrees centigrade or gas mark 6 and bake for another 15 to 20 minutes. The pudding should be deliciously golden brown and well-risen, like this one. Serve the pudding at once.

Pause

Now you will hear the piece again. Rewind the tape and listen.

That is the end of the first part of the test.

SECOND PART

In the second part of the test you will hear an expert answering questions about the marks we find on pieces of silver. Look at questions 14 to 22. Complete the notes by filling in the spaces provided. You will hear the piece twice.

Pause

Tone

David: Wonderful. Makes you feel weak listening to it. It's now time for 'Any answers?' and the first question comes from Peter Wilson, a younger listener in Manchester who writes, 'What do those funny little marks on the backs of spoons or other silver things mean? I've been told that an article is only real silver if there is a little lion stamped on it. Is it true? What should I look for?'
To answer this question, I have my first guest, who is Alan Ball, an expert on English silver. Well Alan, what about Peter's question?

Alan: Well, as we'll see it's partially true but the little lion isn't the only symbol stamped on the pieces. There'll be several more. These little marks are known as 'hallmarks' and to the expert, they tell the history of the piece of silver, the quality, where and when it was made and by whom.

David: Have they been with us a long time?

Alan: Oh yes, our present system dates from 1300 AD when a law came in which fixed the standard for silver as 'sterling'. It stated that 925 parts out of 1,000 must be pure silver. All silver of this standard had to be marked with a leopard's head. This was to stop cheating and there were very heavy penalties if the stamp was misused, erm for example, by putting the stamp on lower quality silver. This law actually lasted till 1856 – over five hundred years.

David: Is this the lion that Peter mentioned?

Alan: No, no, you will usually find four marks on a piece of silver, one of which may be the lion Peter mentioned.

David: What are these marks? Are they easy to recognize? What do they mean?

Alan: Oh yes, yes, they are quite distinctive. The first mark is a town mark. You see, another law made in 1423 AD confirmed the standard of silver and named seven towns to be set up as testing centres. And each town adopted its own mark. Over the years these special centres have changed, and now there are only four – London, Birmingham, Edinburgh and Sheffield. They each have quite distinctive marks. The mark for London is a lion's head, Birmingham uses an anchor, the symbol for Edinburgh is a three-towered castle and Sheffield has used a Tudor Rose since 1975. Before that the mark for Sheffield silver was a crown.

David: Is the town mark a guarantee of quality?

Alan: Yes and no. It shows the silver's been tested. The 'standard' mark which shows the silver is of good quality, is a walking lion and this is the mark Peter mentioned in his question. You see, in 1544, Henry VIII reduced the amount of pure silver in coins, and people thought this would happen to the silver. The lion was introduced to show customers that the silver was 'sterling silver', that is, at least 92.5% pure, and over four hundred years later, people will not believe that a piece is truly silver unless it has the lion on it, although there have sometimes been other 'standard' marks.

David: Can you really tell who made a piece?

Alan: Oh, usually, yes. From very early days makers of silver would put a mark on their own work. In the early days it was a symbol like a sheep's head or a key, but later they used initials or the first two letters of the maker's surname. This is the maker's mark and there are records of the marks used. The other mark which always appears is the date mark. This was, and is, done by adding a letter of the alphabet in a shield, and a different letter is used every year.

David: Isn't that a little confusing?

Alan: Oh no, they use different styles of letters and so on. The combinations are endless and the date mark is never used twice. You do need a book to check the dates though . . .

David: That's quite simple really!

Alan: Well, I've told you part of the story. There have been special standard marks to celebrate special events like the coronation mark of 1953 but the basic system is quite simple. If anyone is interested, there'll be plenty of books on this subject in the local library.

David: Well, thanks to Alan Ball our first guest. Here's another song by . . .

Pause

Now you will hear the piece again. Rewind the tape and listen.

That is the end of the second part of the test.

THIRD PART

In the third part of the test you will hear a guide welcoming a group of tourists to Hong Kong. Look at questions 23 to 33. For questions 23 to 27 complete the notes by filling in the spaces provided. For questions 28 to 33 tick one box to show whether each statement is true or false. You will hear the piece twice.

Pause

Tone

Representative: Good evening, Ladies and Gentlemen. Welcome to Hong Kong. We hope you had a good flight despite the short delay in Dubai and we hope you'll enjoy your stay. It's currently 6.30 p.m. local time and our driver tells me that most of the luggage is now on board and we can leave in a couple of minutes. If you'd like to take out your programme, I'll let you know about one or two changes. First of all, my name is Anna Leung and I'm the local representative for Global Holidays. I'm afraid that Marilyn Chan, whose name is on your programme, is ill so I'll be looking after you. If you want to make a note of my name it's spelt L-E-U-N-G. The journey from the airport which is in Kowloon will take us via the Cross-Harbour Tunnel to the Mandarin Hotel which is on Hong Kong Island. This journey should take us about half an hour if there isn't too much traffic. As we are just a little late, the welcome drinks in the Captain's Bar will now be at

7.30 p.m. rather than 7.00. All your rooms are on the ninth and tenth floors and you can pick up your keys from reception as soon as you arrive in the hotel. The registration forms have been completed on your behalf so just give the receptionist your name and sign the form.

If you want to rest then dinner will be at 8.30 rather than 8.00 p.m. for this evening only.

I will be in the lobby of the hotel for an hour from 7.00 p.m. every evening so please come and see me if you have any problems or queries. If you want to contact me during the day you can leave a message for me at the office of Lucky Tours who are the local agents for Global Travel. Oh, the number is on your information sheet. A full programme of each day's activities will be on our notice board in the hotel. I'll point it out to you as we go in. Just let me remind you however, that your first excursion, which is a bus tour of Hong Kong island, starts at 2.15 tomorrow afternoon so please be in the lobby of the hotel about five minutes before. Finally, as we still have a moment I'd just like to mention that Thursday is a free day on your programme but it is the fifth day of the fifth moon in the lunar calendar and this is a very important Chinese festival known as the Dragon Boat Festival. You see, several centuries before the birth of Christ, a poet drowned himself in the river to protest against the government of his times. The boatmen raced to his help but they couldn't get there so they threw rice in the river so that the fish would not eat his body. Nowadays we eat special rice dumplings and have dragon boat races to frighten away the fish. As you'll see these boats are very colourful and the races are very noisy and exciting. There will be a special excursion to the races leaving at 10 a.m. on Thursday. The excursion will return to the hotel by about 6.30 p.m. and lunch is included in the price of HK$150 (one hundred and fifty Hong Kong Dollars). If you are interested please let me know by tomorrow evening. Right, our driver tells me that all the luggage is now on and we're ready to leave. Do you have any questions?

Pause

Now you will hear the piece again. Rewind the tape and listen.

That is the end of the third part of the test. There will now be a pause to allow you to check your work.

Pause

Tone

That is the end of the test.

PAPER 5   INTERVIEW   (15 to 20 minutes)

SECTION B   PASSAGES FOR COMMENT

Suggested answers:

1   a) Spoken or written (an informal letter)
    b) Somebody who is telling a friend about a job s/he did in the past.
        S/he was probably quite young at the time.
    c) The passage gives details of a dreadful place to work.

2   a) Spoken
    b) An unemployed person having a conversation with someone
    c) The speaker is telling somebody how difficult it is to get a job.

3   a) Written
    b) A careers advice service advertising in a newspaper or magazine to people in senior
        jobs
    c) The advice service is offering to help people find more fulfilling jobs.

See Introduction for marking criteria for Interview paper.

Total = 30 marks   Pass = 18 marks

PRACTICE TEST 3

PAPER 1   READING COMPREHENSION   (1 hour)

SECTION A   1 mark for each correct answer

1 C	6 B	11 A	16 B	21 C
2 D	7 C	12 D	17 A	22 D
3 C	8 B	13 D	18 A	23 A
4 D	9 A	14 C	19 D	24 D
5 B	10 B	15 B	20 C	25 A

SECTION B   2 marks for each correct answer

26 B	31 C	36 B
27 D	32 A	37 C
28 B	33 C	38 C
29 A	34 D	39 B
30 C	35 B	40 D

Total = 55 marks   Pass = about 33 marks

PAPER 2   COMPOSITION   (1½ hours)

See Introduction for marking criteria.

Total = 40 marks   Pass = about 16 marks

PAPER 3   USE OF ENGLISH   (2 hours)

1   1 mark for each correct answer

1	at		12	in
2	had		13	told
3	of		14	last
4	advertisement/advert		15	to
5	for		16	was
6	(al)though/but		17	who
7	got		18	whether/if
8	later/after		19	another
9	wear		20	been
10	along			
11	On			Total = 20 marks

2   Give marks as shown for sections in italics

    a   I apologize *for interrupting* your dinner.   2
    b   My purse *was stolen* from my handbag.   2
    c   She told *John to go home* at once.   2
    d   The weather *was so good* that we went swimming.   2
    e   He *isn't interested in getting* a new job.   2
    f   The garden isn't *big enough* to play football in.   2
    g   How long *have you been working* here?   2
    h   It's time *that the children were* in bed/*for the children to be* in bed.   2
    i   She is *the youngest* in the group.   2
    j   There's *nothing he can do* about it.   2

Total = 20 marks

3   1 mark for each correct answer

    a   dishonest
    b   unnecessary
    c   nonsense
    d   unhopeful
    e   improbable

Total = 5 marks

4   Give marks as shown for suitable responses and correct punctuation

    a   That sounds the sort of place/sounds fine. How do you/we/I get there?   4
    b   How often do the buses run?   2
    c   (And) how long does it take?   2
    d   Can you tell me when it is open/the Pavilion is open/it/the Pavilion opens, please?   2
    e   Is it expensive (to get in)?   2
    f   (That's a lot as) we have (two) children.   3
    g   That's a good idea. Thank you (very much).   4 + 1 for writing two sentences.

Total = 20 marks

5   In this question the student should be able to choose relevant material and then present the facts in a reasonably fluent form.

Any choice may be made but good reasons should be offered for the choice.

The answer should contain carefully chosen information, written in a continuous style, but should not be too long.

Give 15 marks for the piece of writing, taking into account the above points.

The following are notes for a suggested answer:

Crossings could be where two traffic lights are already: linking centre of village and shops. Save money because lights already there. Two crossings – one across Bradford Road and one across York Road, would also link York Road estate and Bradford Estate through centre. Also safer access to children's playground and park.

Charlton Road quite quiet, so no need for crossing there. Crossing outside school would only be useful for children, not adults.

Total = 15 marks

Final total = 80 marks   Pass = about 40 marks

PAPER 4   LISTENING COMPREHENSION   (about 30 minutes)

FIRST PART   ½ mark for each correct answer

1	T	7	F
2	F	8	T
3	T	9	F
4	F	10	F
5	F	11	F
6	T		

Total = 5½ marks

SECOND PART   1 mark for each correct answer

OSCARS   Sales Note

Order no: (12) 5 4 7 8 1
Customer's Name: (13) De Freitas
Address: 6, Anville way, Cambridge CB1 5E2
Telephone number: (14) 0932 243023

(15)

Description	Code	Price
All items black:		
4 drawer chest	C G 02631	£ 420
(a) 6 drawer		(e) ---------
60 cm bedside unit	C6 02630	£ 160 - 10
Dressing - table top	C6 02610	£ 90 - 40
	(c) C6 02605	
220 cm wardrobe	C6 02618	£ 1,402 - 50
		(f) £ 894 - 30
2 door cupboard	C36 02692	£ 247 - 50
(b) ---------------	(d) C6 02692	

Delivery notes:
(16) Key with Mrs. Jones at Number 4
....

Registered office: Oscar & Son Ltd, 296 New Court Road,
London W3 6FV

Total = 8 marks

THIRD PART   Give marks as shown

17	1 metre	½ mark		21	wooden	1 mark
18	2 metres	½ mark		22	water	1 mark
19	(top of the) fishing net	1 mark		23	A	½ mark
20	(main) ropes	1 mark		24	C	½ mark
				25	11 metres	½ mark

Total = 6½ marks

Final total = 20 marks

Tapescript

FIRST PART

For the first part of the test you will hear part of a holiday programme on the radio. Look at questions 1 to 11.

Tick one box to show whether each answer is true or false. You will hear the piece twice.

Pause

Tone

First presenter:	Winter World is giving a discount for people who book early and that's worth £17 for one week and £23 for two. Now all the prices are guaranteed so you won't pay any more than the price in the brochure and I hope that all the other companies follow this lead so there will be no surcharges. Winter World have got twenty-six new resorts in this year's brochure so there's a lot to choose from. They also have luxury winter holidays for skiers who want the best hotels and holiday makers who don't ski but like the Alps in winter.
	Another company you might look at is Olsens. They have quite a few interesting things in their brochure. First there are some £59-a-week skiing holidays. Secondly they do skiing holidays for the over-55s.
Second presenter:	Over-55s?
First presenter:	Oh yes, you can have a very good holiday even if you're over 50. If you get expert tuition and only use the gentle slopes it's great fun. I don't know why people think skiing is only for young people. It's not. You can have a marvellous holiday.
Second presenter:	How about insurance?
First presenter:	Insurance and everything else is the same. They're well worth it.
	They also have holidays for youngsters from 13 to 17 who go alone. And the other nice thing is that they've got this offer where if you've never been skiing before and the holiday is a disaster and despite taking lessons you just can't ski you get £50 back.
Second presenter:	Sounds marvellous.

First presenter: Olsens and Winter World are skiing specialists so if you fancy a winter holiday in the *sun* you might look at Worldwide winter programme which comes out on Monday. They're the big one now you know with between 30 and 50% of the market. They too will give discounts to people who book early rather than reductions for late bookings and some of their prices will be incredibly low. In addition to a normal winter programme you'll find that they have a lot of self-catering holidays for people who have plenty of time to go away for some winter sun. So if you've just retired you might be interested in a self-catering holiday in some small holiday flats in Benidorm. The ten weeks, that's seventy nights, will cost £139 including the flight. That's about two pounds a day! But you get what you pay for and you might prefer to try something that's just a little bit better, with a little more luxury. So for example there's Worldwide's own two star hotel the Park in Marbella. Four weeks there. That's twenty-eight nights, £232 for full board including excursions. That works out at about £8.00 a day. Still cheap.

Second presenter: Can't wait till I'm 65.

First presenter: Now if the lovely weather we've been having lately makes you decide to stay at home you might be interested in a new company that deals in holidays in Britain . . .

Pause

Now you will hear the piece again. Rewind the tape and listen.

That is the end of the first part of the test.

SECOND PART

In the second part of the test you will hear a telephone conversation about a furniture order. Look at questions 12 to 16. For questions 12 to 14 and question 16, write the information on the appropriate part of the form. For question 15 make 4, and only 4, changes in the spaces provided. You will hear the piece twice.

Pause

Tone

Telephonist: Good afternoon, Oscars.

Customer: Good afternoon. Could I speak to bedroom furniture please?

Telephonist: Hold the line.

Salesperson: Bedding!

Customer: Er, could I speak to Miss Wilson, please.

Salesperson: I'm afraid Monday's her day off. Can I help you?

Customer:	Well I'm afraid there were one or two errors in the order I placed on Saturday and I wanted to put it right.
Salesperson:	That's no problem. I can dig the order out. Can I have your name please?
Customer:	Yes. It's De Freitas. That's spelt D-E and then F-R-E-I-T-A-S, De Freitas. Would you like the order number?
Salesperson:	That would be very helpful.
Customer:	It's 5–4–7–8–1.
Salesperson:	Just hang on a second while I have a look . . . Ah yes. Here we are. What seems to be the problem?
Customer:	The first problem is that we've been overcharged. You've charged us £1402.50 for the 220cm wardrobe! Well we had a look at the catalogue when we got home and that's the price for a 240cm wardrobe. The price should be £894.30.
Salesperson:	Well I'll make a note and check it. Were there any other problems?
Customer:	Yes. I'm afraid there were. If you have a look at the order you'll see there's a chest code number C6 02631. Can you find it?
Salesperson:	Yes.
Customer:	Well it should be a six drawer chest. I expect your girl made a mistake. She seemed to be very new and wasn't at all sure what to do. In fact she's even got one item marked as C36 when it should be C6. C36 is for white and we've ordered black! And that would be a slight problem. Wouldn't it?
Salesperson:	Don't worry, we'll get it right . . .
Customer:	There's just one other small problem. We've had another look at our bedroom and we are afraid the 180cm dressing-table top is just not going to fit so could we go for the smaller one? Its number is C6 02605. OK?
Salesperson:	Yes, I'm sure that'll be fine. I'll get Miss Wilson to reprocess the order when she gets in tomorrow. Is there a number we can call you at during the day?
Customer:	Yes, you can reach me at Walton, that's 0932 from London, 243023. Just ask for the Sales Office. You will send me a copy of the revised order?
Salesperson:	Yes, it should be in the post to you by the end of the week. I'm sorry for the problems. I'm sure we'll sort them out.
Customer:	Just one last thing. My wife and I are out most of the day so I was wondering if you could get the delivery men to call for a key at Mrs Jones who lives at Number 4. She'll let them in.
Salesperson:	OK. I'll just make a note of that on the form and we'll be in touch to confirm the order.
Customer:	Many thanks. Goodbye.

Pause

Now you will hear the piece again. Rewind the tape and listen.

That is the end of the second part of the test.

THIRD PART

In the third part of the test you will hear a radio talk about a boat. Look at questions 17 to 25. Fill in the missing information in the spaces provided. You will hear the piece twice.

Pause

Tone

Presenter: There is a form of fishing – and fishing boat – that has not changed for thousands of years and which is still used in Wales today. The boat is known as a coracle and it is very easy to recognize because it has a very unusual and distinctive shape for a boat. It looks like half an egg, with a seat across the centre of it. It's usually about 1 metre to 1 metre 50 wide and about 1 metre 70 to 2 metres long, but the measurements do vary because coracles are made for the person who is going to use them.

There are still one or two made in the old traditional way. Originally, the outside covering was animal skin. In fact, the cow played a very important part in the making of a coracle. The coracle had a wooden frame, and this frame was covered by cowhide, which was stretched tightly over the frame. Once the hide was on, it had to be made waterproof, and cow fat was used to stop water getting in. The coracle was usually used for fishing so the cow's horns, which are hollow, were cut up into rings for the top of the fishing net. And hair from the cow's tail was also used to spin the main ropes. Today, it's more convenient to use modern materials. Ropes are made of polythene and nylon, and the external covering of most coracles is made of fibreglass, but the shape and design of the boat remains the same. This is because the coracle is very easy to manoeuvre and the boat is controlled by a single paddle. The person in the boat sits so that the round end is in the front but the main advantage of the coracle is that it moves sideways.

The sideways movement of a coracle makes it ideal for river fishing. The men work in pairs. They move slowly down the river with the tide and use an 11 metre long net to try to catch salmon as they go up-river to produce their young. The salmon swim very near the bottom and so any net which is more than about half a metre from the bottom of the river would not catch them. If you row as you would in an ordinary boat, the net would be pulled away from the bottom each time you moved and many of the fish would swim under. The coracle however, moves very slowly, and the net stays at the bottom where it is wanted. Coracle fishing takes a long time because you can catch only one fish at a time. This is because the net is very light and as soon as a fish swims into it the net will wrap itself round the fish. The only way you can catch more than one is if the fish reach the net at the same speed.

Coracle fishing is dying out. At one time there used to be thousands of men coracle fishing but today only a handful still use this ancient boat.

Unfortunately modern methods catch many more salmon so the coracle is now inefficient. Unfortunately, as fewer fish get up-river to produce their young, there is a danger that all salmon fishing could disappear from Wales soon. When that happens the coracle might disappear as well.

Pause

Now you will hear the piece again. Rewind the tape and listen.

That is the end of the third part of the test.

There will now be a pause to allow you to check your work.

Pause
Tone

That is the end of the test.

PAPER 5   INTERVIEW   (15 to 20 minutes)

SECTION B   PASSAGES FOR COMMENT

Suggested answers:

1 a) Spoken
   b) A disc-jockey on the radio
   c) The speaker is telling people about records that have just come into the shops.

2 a) Could be written or spoken (perhaps an article in a newspaper or an informative radio programme)
   b) A researcher; somebody who knows a lot about TV viewing habits of Americans
   c) The researcher is talking about TV viewing in the U.S.A.

3 a) Spoken (for a radio programme) or written (perhaps an autobiography?)
   b) An actor or actress
   c) S/he is talking about the past, possibly when s/he was a child, and the way s/he used to go to the theatre with his/her mother.

See Introduction for marking criteria for Interview paper.

Total = 30 marks   Pass = about 18 marks

PRACTICE TEST 4

PAPER 1   READING COMPREHENSION   (1 hour)

SECTION A   1 mark for each correct answer

1	C	6	B	11	A	16	A	21	D
2	B	7	B	12	D	17	B	22	C
3	A	8	A	13	C	18	B	23	A
4	A	9	C	14	D	19	C	24	B
5	D	10	C	15	B	20	B	25	C

SECTION B   2 marks for each correct answer

26	B	31	C	36	C
27	C	32	D	37	A
28	A	33	C	38	D
29	D	34	B	39	A
30	B	35	D	40	D

Total = 55 marks   Pass = about 33 marks

PAPER 2   COMPOSITION   (1½ hours)

See Introduction for marking criteria.

Total = 40 marks   Pass = about 16 marks

PAPER 3   USE OF ENGLISH   (2 hours)

1   One mark for each correct answer

1	who	12	by
2	their	13	loudly
3	getting	14	(Al)though
4	spend	15	made
5	the	16	into
6	none	17	neither
7	old	18	so
8	in	19	tell/answer
9	over	20	on
10	would/should		
11	packed		Total = 20 marks

2   Give marks as shown for sections in italics

    a   I *lent him my book*, but he forgot to return it.   2
    b   He was *made to wait* for two hours.   2
    c   I will miss the bus *if I don't leave* now/*unless I leave* now.   2
    d   It is *too far (for me)* to see.   2
    e   She drives *more slowly and carefully than me*/I do.   2
    f   For two months now the police *have been looking* for him.   2
    g   When do you think (that) this house *was built*?   2
    h   It's *such an expensive holiday*, that I don't think I can go.   2
    i   Not only *is it* the cheapest watch, but *it's also the nicest.*   2
    j   I'll give you a ring *when I get home* at about seven.   2

Total = 20 marks

3   1 mark for each correct answer

    a   slow
    b   hours
    c   dawn/daybreak
    d   days
    e   season

Total = 5 marks

4   Give marks as shown for sections in italics

    a   *I'm/was* sorry *to hear* (that) the/your car *is/has been giving* (you) trouble again.   3
    b   *Does that/it mean* (that) *you won't be able to go camping* in July?   3
    c   I *told* you when *you bought it* (that) it *was a mistake* to buy *something/one* so cheap.   4
    d   *After paying* garage bills etc. cheaper cars *are* more expensive.   2
    e   My news is that *I have/I've changed* my job and I *now work for/am working for* the local newspaper.   3
    f   I *got tired of* the/my old job and the pay *wasn't* very good.   2
    g   *I am in charge of* the car advertisement section *in/of the* newspaper.   2
    h   *Shall I try to* find a better car *for* you?   2

Total = 21 marks

5   In this question the student should be able to choose relevant material and then present the facts in a reasonably fluent form.

    Any choice may be made but good reasons should be offered for the choice.

    The answer should contain carefully chosen information, written in a continuous style, but should not be too long.

    Give 7 marks for each paragraph.

    The following notes suggest some possible reasons for the choices:

    The best solution would be . . . Suggestion 3. Kitchen is large enough to eat in and therefore no need for dining-room.

Play-room etc. near kitchen so parent could keep an eye on children. Also near garden and away from main road. Play-room could also become another bedroom as children become bigger.

The least satisfactory solution would be . . . Suggestion 1. Both bedrooms would be very small and second largest room as dining-room seems a waste of space.

Total = 14 marks

Final total = 80 marks   Pass = about 40 marks

PAPER 4   LISTENING COMPREHENSION   (about 30 minutes)

FIRST PART   1½ marks for each correct answer

1 B   4 A
2 D   5 D
3 C

Total = 7½ marks

SECOND PART   1½ marks for each correct answer

6 A 3   D 5
   B 6   E 2
   C 4

Total = 7½ marks

THIRD PART   ½ mark for each correct answer

7   over 1,000   12 No
8   1986   13 Yes
9   60%   14 No
10 12 months   15 No
11 9 months (½ mark)
    4 years   (½ mark)

Total = 5 marks

Final total = 20 marks

Tapescript

FIRST PART

For the first part of the test you will hear an expert talking about how the police use photofit pictures. Look at questions 1 to 5. For each question put a tick in one of the boxes A, B, C or D to show the correct answer. You will hear the piece twice.

Pause

Tone

Interviewer:	On our screens over the past few weeks we've seen a number of likenesses of criminals that the police want to interview. We ask the questions are there too many and do they really look like the criminals? In our studio this morning we have Professor Alex Jones who has been doing research in this area. Alex, how do the police get the 'pictures' we see?
Expert:	Well, the police use a variety of methods to try and capture a true likeness. Most of the police use a system called photofit. This is a sort of jigsaw puzzle, and they try and build up the face out of a series of pictures of separate facial features.
	But sometimes pictures are built up with the help of artists. Artists working with the witness help them to produce a likeness which aims to be really life-like. Now there's some controversy as to whether photofits or artist's impressions are better. I think the police believe in trying both. After all you might get something . . .
Interviewer:	Yes, now staying with photofits, tell me, how are they actually made up?
Expert:	Well, the witness gives a general description and then the policeman trained to use the photofit goes to his kit of parts where he has five hundred and fifty different pictures of parts of the face. These cover five different features: the hairline, the eyes, the nose, the mouth and the chin, and on . . . on the basis of the description the operator will let the witness choose the different parts to produce an overall impression. If there are any special distinguishing marks such as scars, he can add these with the help of a wax pencil . . . so the face is literally built up from different parts. Just like a jigsaw.
Interviewer:	I see, tell me, am I right in thinking that there must be problems in using photofit?
Expert:	Oh yes, I mean there are problems in using any system. If the picture is put together after the witness has only seen the person for a very short time and there is a long delay before the subject is interviewed, photofit will produce a likeness which is not very good at all. It would be at best what we call a 'type' likeness, that is, it would be a general likeness which might be any one of several thousand people and a great deal of time can be wasted as the police investigate all the reports which come in. The best pictures are when the witness has had a chance to look at the criminal for some time, for example during a conversation. The lighting conditions are also very important. A lot of crime takes place at night and of course it's not easy to get a good impression of a face under street lights or in dark doorways . . .

Interviewer: Yes indeed. Tell me, is photofit in colour?

Expert: No, no, it's not at present. Photofit is still very simple and all the different photographs of parts of the face have to be put on pieces of card and so on. It's still quite old-fashioned but there should be big developments soon as a result of computer technology and scientists are working on a system where witnesses will be able to work alone and build up colour pictures on a computer monitor in their own home.

Interviewer: Well, that sounds like something for the future. But what about the present? How can we make the photofit system work better now?

Expert: Well, we need a range of pictures to capture the range of faces we're likely to see in Britain, including foreign nationals, and more trained operators in every police station as we're short of these. It's also a problem keeping the kits up to date as fashion changes a lot these days. If you think of all the new styles of hair for men and women, you can see it's really quite a job keeping up with it all . . .

Interviewer: Yes, indeed. So do you think we should forget about photofit and just use the old-fashioned artist?

Expert: No, I don't think so. The system does have its faults but as long as we're aware of them we can use it and even if we only catch one criminal then you could argue that it's still worth it.

Interviewer: Thank you very much, Professor Jones, for . . .

Pause

Now you will hear the piece again. Rewind the tape and listen.

That is the end of the first part of the test.

SECOND PART

In the second part of the test you will hear a talk about cities in the future. Look at question 6. For question 6, number the diagrams in the order they are mentioned. For example, diagram F is mentioned first so you write 1 in the box. You will hear the piece twice.

Pause

Tone

Architect: Thank you very much for asking me here to talk to your environmental group. My subject for tonight is 'Cities of the world—problems and solutions'. I'd like to start by showing you a few drawings of cities that architects have invented. I shall then allow for questions and discussion before we explore ways in which some of the problems of our own town can be overcome. One of the big problems in the modern world is population growth. In India alone, over twelve million babies are born every year. Some experts are worried that in about two hundred years there will not be enough to eat, raw materials will disappear, and we shall all be living in an enormous suburb of a world city. Not everyone accepts this but architects have been thinking of cities for an overpopulated world and I'd like to start by showing you some designs.

The first drawing we're going to look at is not new. In the 1920s, the famous American architect, Frank Lloyd Wright, planned a city called Broadacre. At that time, nobody worried about overpopulation and Wright believed that industrial cities were not the best way for people to live and so he put his ideal city in the middle of green fields. Space was unlimited and each family had its own house and car. You can see Lloyd Wright's influence in many of the new housing developments surrounding some of our cities but in many places they are a threat to the countryside and architects have more recently tried to find other places to build.

The Italian architect, Paolo Soleri, thought a good place for a city would be where there are very few people at present so he chose the desert. This isn't as strange as it looks; most deserts were green and fertile at one time. It is only that they became hotter and drier so that few things could grow there. Soleri decided that a system of dams and canals would soon change that. He called his concept 'Mesa City' and saw it as a system of thirty-four villages which are all connected to the centre.

William Katavolos, an American architect, thought on similar lines and so he designed a floating city to make use of the space in the sea. His floating city is made of a new kind of plastic which goes hard when it touches water and the city is a number of artificial islands connected to each other.

Some others have been less revolutionary. A French architect, Edouard Utudjian, decided that in his city, all the factories, cars, railways etc. would go underground and only people would live on the surface. Here there would be no roads, only woods and fields.

In another way of saving space, the Swiss architect, Walter Jonas, decided to leave as much room as possible on the ground for trees and fields, and so designed units which were over 100 metres high and shaped like a funnel – i.e. narrow at the bottom and wide at the top.

Another architect, the Frenchman, Paul Maymont, was more worried about ruining old cities than finding new places so he planned huge suspended platforms, which looked like trees. Each platform would contain shops, flats and offices. They could be connected to each other and the old city.

Perhaps the strangest idea was invented by the English architect, Reg Herron. Herron decided that there would be one capital of the world, which he planned as a huge engine. The other cities would look like large machines on gigantic mechanical legs, and they would take the cities wherever they were needed.

I think these suggestions can help solve some of our problems. Today, there are serious attempts to make the desert live again and many cities have gone underground, but perhaps some of you have questions and comments at this point.

Pause

Now you will hear the piece again. Rewind the tape and listen.

That is the end of the second part of the test.

THIRD PART

In the third part of the test you will hear an announcement about safety in cars. Look at questions 7 to 15. For questions 7 to 11 complete the missing information in the spaces provided. For questions 12 to 15 tick the boxes to show if what is illustrated is recommended or not. You will hear the piece twice.

Pause

Tone

Speaker: Protect your child. Loose objects in a car get thrown about or damaged in an accident. Your child could be that object. An accident can mean serious injury or death, even at low speed, and every year over a thousand children are killed or seriously injured by being thrown about in a car, so make sure your child is protected.

       The law requires all passengers (adults, babies and children) to wear a restraint like a seat belt when they travel in the front of a car and since October 1986 all new cars have had to have rear seat belts or child restraints, so it makes sense to protect your children when they are sitting in the front *and* the back. After all, using these can reduce the risk of injury by about sixty per cent.

       You can now buy specially made restraints to suit all ages and sizes of children so make sure you get the right thing for your child.

       Young babies aged up to twelve months should have a safety seat that faces the rear of the car so that the baby has extra support in an accident. The special baby seats can be used in either the front or the back seat and may be held in place by an adult seat belt.

       If this is impossible, very small babies can travel in a carry-cot. This can function as a bed for the baby and the handles make it easy to carry around but you have to make sure it is used correctly. If you use a carry-cot you should make sure you have straps to stop the cot from falling off the back seat. If that is impossible, place the cot on the floor between the front and back seats. A folded blanket will help to make the floor level and stop the cot from moving. Try to place the baby's head near the middle of the car and make sure there is a cover on the carry-cot to stop the baby from being thrown out of the top.

       For children between nine months and four years of age a child safety seat is recommended. The child cannot move about the car and there is side support so that the child can sleep. Many child seats are fixed to the body of the car. Others may be held in place by an adult seat strap and they are easy to use. For older children we suggest a lap belt and two shoulder straps or a special cushion to raise the height of the child so that an adult belt can be used. This special cushion is made with hooks or straps to hold it in place and you should never use an ordinary household cushion because it could let the child slip out of the belt. Most child belts or seats can be bought for less than £40 and those that can be attached to adult seat belts can be installed very quickly and cheaply.

       If you haven't got rear child restraints yet, make sure you choose the type suited to your children and car. The restraint or seat belt should fit the child well. Whatever you do, never carry a child on your knee and don't let children stand in the gap between the front seats or on the rear seats. Remember, it's always better to be safe than sorry.

Pause

Now you will hear the piece again. Rewind the tape and listen.

This is the end of the third part of the test. There will now be a pause to allow you to check your work.

Pause

Tone

That is the end of the test.

PAPER 5   INTERVIEW   (15 to 20 minutes)

SECTION B   PASSAGES FOR COMMENT

Suggested answers:

1 a) Could be written or spoken
   b) Somebody who knows about security matters
   c) The person is giving advice about what you should do if you think your car has been stolen.

2 a) Probably written in a popular newspaper, or a book of amusing stories
   b) A journalist or writer
   c) Somebody telling an amusing story of a rather amateur bank robber, who didn't really know how to set about robbing the bank.

3 a) Probably written in a magazine
   b) Somebody who has been robbed a few times
   c) S/he tells about his/her latest experience of being robbed.

See Introduction for marking criteria for Interview paper.

Total = 30 marks   Pass = about 18 marks

PRACTICE TEST 5

PAPER 1   READING COMPREHENSION   (1 hour)

SECTION A   1 mark for each correct answer

1	D	6	C	11	D	16	A	21	B
2	D	7	B	12	B	17	C	22	D
3	A	8	C	13	C	18	B	23	B
4	A	9	A	14	B	19	A	24	A
5	B	10	D	15	A	20	A	25	D

SECTION B   2 marks for each correct answer

26	B	31	B	36	C
27	B	32	C	37	A
28	D	33	C	38	B
29	A	34	C	39	A
30	C	35	A	40	D

Total = 55 marks   Pass = about 33 marks

PAPER 2   COMPOSITION   (1½ hours)

See Introduction for marking criteria.

Total = 40 marks   Pass = about 16 marks

PAPER 3   USE OF ENGLISH   (2 hours)

1   1 mark for each correct answer

1	just/only	12	such
2	but	13	could
3	had	14	did
4	than	15	on
5	instead	16	All
6	of	17	believe
7	height	18	even
8	with	19	straight
9	later/after	20	something
10	drive		
11	glances/looks	Total = 20 marks	

2   Give marks as shown for sections in italics

    a   We were *happier than ever* before/*than we had ever been* before.   2
    b   I regret *not learning*/*not having learnt* to ride a bike when I was younger.   2
    c   The boat *was made to turn back* by the police.   4
    d   It's the first time that *I've ever been* to the ballet.   2
    e   He spoke too quickly *for me to understand* what he said.   2
    f   Please *repeat what you said*, John, she said.   2
    g   The reason she lost her job *was that* she didn't work hard enough.   2
    h   Thank you *for looking after* my mother so well.   2
    i   The traffic makes it *impossible to cross* the road.   2
    j   He wasn't tall *enough to reach* the switch.   2

Total = 22 marks

3   1 mark for each correct answer

    a   dish
    b   courses
    c   recipe
    d   diet
    e   taste/flavour

Total = 5 marks

4   Give marks as shown for sections in italics

    a   It *became*/*has become* so expensive (that) I *can't afford* to live there.   3
    b   How much *was your* last electricity bill?   1
    c   Our/My last bill *came to* over £200.   1
    d   *The*/*My*/*Our flat* is very cold so I/we *spend a lot on* heating.   2
    e   *I've been looking for* a new flat *for* three weeks now but I can't find *one*/*anything*.   3
    f   *Can*/*Will you mention it* to your friends *at*/*in the* office?   2
    g   *It's a waste of time looking in the* newspapers.   4
    h   *The good ones*/*flats always go* by the time I telephone/*have always gone* by the time I telephone.   2

Total = 18 marks

5   In this question the student should be able to choose relevant material and then present the facts in a reasonably fluent form.

Any choice may be made, but good reasons should be offered for the choice.

The answer should contain carefully chosen information written in a continuous style, but should not be too long.

Give 5 marks for each of the paragraphs.

The following notes suggest some possible reasons:

I would suggest as first choice . . . charter/flight. This is medium price and a short journey for the young children. Advance booking should be possible.

I would suggest as second choice . . . train/boat. Although long journey for children they can move about and it's a new experience. Plenty of choice about time to travel. Own carriage on the train?

I would not suggest . . . scheduled flight as this is much too expensive. Coach/boat means the children could not move about and might become bored and tired before they arrived.

Total = 15 marks

Final total = 80 marks   Pass = about 40 marks

PAPER 4   LISTENING COMPREHENSION   (about 30 minutes)

FIRST PART

½ mark for each correct answer

1	F	5	F
2	T	6	F
3	F	7	T
4	T		

1 mark for each correct answer

8 a) telephone the police
   b) shout for help
9 a) his instructions
   b) get away

Total = 7½ marks

SECOND PART   Give marks as shown

10   D 293 JFL   1½ marks
11   20,000   ½ mark
12   front passenger (1 mark) inside (½ mark)
13   Thursday 23 July   1 mark
14   Yes   ½ mark
15   No   ½ mark
16   5 pm   ½ mark

Total = 6 marks

THIRD PART ½ mark for each box ticked as shown below and also ½ mark for each box without a tick as shown below. Do not include box b) as this was given in the question.

Advice given

a)	Hire a large van.		h)	Arrange to connect your washing machine.	
b)	Use a removal firm.	✓	i)	If packing yourself, collect containers in supermarkets.	✓
c)	Get more than one estimate.	✓	j)	Don't pack all your books in one box.	✓
d)	Move at weekends.		k)	Protect fragile things.	✓
e)	Send your children away.	✓	l)	Pack everything you need.	
f)	Pack little boxes yourself.		m)	Label all your boxes.	
g)	Read your meter before you move.	✓	n)	Clean up before you go.	✓

Total = 6½ marks

Final total = 20 marks

Tapescript

FIRST PART

For the first part of the test you will hear part of a talk by a policeman. Look at questions 1 to 9. For questions 1 to 7 tick one box to show whether you think each statement is true or false. For questions 8 and 9 complete the missing information in the spaces provided. You will hear the piece twice.

Pause

Tone

Good evening. It was very good of you to invite me to speak to you tonight. As Madam Chairman said I'm based at your local police station where I'm the crime prevention officer. I suppose you're fed up with experts telling you how to prevent crises so er what I'd like to do tonight is to give you a few words of advice on what to do if you find yourself the victim of one of the crimes that are affecting more and more of us. After that I'll give you a chance for questions and discussion and then if we have time we'll perhaps end the session with some ideas on how to prevent these crimes in the first place. I'd like to start with burglary. Unfortunately more and more people are affected by this. Thefts from the home have been increasing dramatically. This year one in ten British homes will be broken into. In fact, last year in London alone there were 168,900 burglaries which is 461 a day or one every three minutes. No doubt later on some of you who are here tonight will be able to tell us about burglaries that you have experienced or heard about.

Now many of us think of the burglar as a professional who works at night stealing expensive jewellery and antiques from stately homes and mansions where the rich live. This couldn't be further from the truth. You're just as likely to be burgled in a small flat as a big house and in fact some 40% of burglaries are committed during the day, often by youngsters who take the opportunity to steal because they see a way in – an open door or window. In fact the great majority of burglars are amateurs who only steal two or three times in their lives. So what do you do if you arrive home and find someone in your house? Different people react in different ways. Some of you may have heard the story of the 86-year-old woman who chased two youngsters out of her house with an umbrella. Well, my advice to you is don't try it! There may be more of them than you can see and if you attack them you might get hurt. It's money and valuables they're after, not you. Don't scream either, or you might make the intruder panic and attack you. If you keep your distance and remain quiet he'll probably drop everything and leave and then you can get the police. Remember, there may be valuable clues so don't touch anything before they arrive. Sometimes you can spot the signs of a break-in before you go in – a broken lock with the chain across the door or a broken window. If you think there's someone inside don't go in. Phone the police from the nearest telephone and with any luck they'll catch him.

You really should adopt a similar approach if someone wakes you up at night. If the thief is actually in your bedroom your best bet is to lie perfectly still and allow the burglar time to leave before you ring the police. If you hear a burglar in another part of the house it's still the safest thing to do but if you have a secure door you could lock yourself in and then telephone the police or shout for help from the bedroom window. Don't go looking for him with a stick or a heavy metal object like a poker – it may make you feel better but it could be used against you.

Another crime which is steadily increasing is street robbery. Although the streets are still quite safe if you're sensible and avoid deserted and badly lit areas. However if you're walking alone and someone leaps out from a doorway and grabs your bag what should you do? Well the first thing as always is to remain calm and let go of the bag. Then try and scream as loudly as you can. This should frighten the thief and might bring help. Forget about hitting back with tins of gas or kicking the thief, there probably won't be time, and unless you're very tough and strong you're not likely to win. If the robber has a weapon you should just keep calm and follow his instructions and give him time to get away. I suppose the crime that most women would fear most is . . .

Pause

Now you will hear the piece again. Rewind the tape and listen.

That is the end of the first part of the test.

SECOND PART

In the second part of the test you will hear a telephone conversation between a woman and a man at a garage. Look at questions 10 to 17. For questions 10 to 17 complete the information on the form. You will hear the piece twice.

Pause
Tone

Receptionist:	Bennet's Garage Ltd. Can I help you?
Customer:	Er, yes. I'd like to book a service for my car please.
Receptionist:	Fine. Have you been to us before?
Customer:	Yes.
Receptionist:	Right just give me your registration number please.
Customer:	My er . . . Oh yes it's D 293 JFL.
Receptionist:	D 293 JFL. Sorry to keep you waiting, it's the computer. Ah yes. Mrs Stevens isn't it? What kind of service is it?
Customer:	Well it's coming up to 20,000 miles so as we're going to the Continent the week after we thought we'd get it done now.
Receptionist:	Is there anything else you'd like us to do?
Customer:	Just let me think. No, the car is basically alright, I think . . . Oh yes, the front passenger door doesn't close properly and I've been having trouble with the inside light. It sometimes comes on without warning but nothing serious . . .
Receptionist:	Right. I'll make a note of these. When would you like to bring the car in? How about Monday of next week?
Customer:	Er, that's not ideal. I have a business meeting in London that day. How about Wednesday?
Receptionist:	I'm sorry we can't manage Wednesday. We're very busy at the moment as it's just before the holidays. I'm afraid it's Monday or Thursday.
Customer:	OK. Make it Thursday.
Receptionist:	Fine, see you at 8.30 on Thursday 23 July then.
Customer:	Oh yes! Will you have a courtesy car? I'll need a car to get around in for the day . . .
Receptionist:	I think we might be able to help. Hang on a moment. I'll just check. That'll be fine. Just pick up the keys from reception. Oh by the way would you like us to adjust your headlights for driving on the Continent? It won't cost you anything.
Customer:	Erm no, I'll do it myself just before I go. I might need the car at night. Just one last thing. When will the car be ready?
Receptionist:	What time would you like it?
Customer:	5 p.m.?
Receptionist:	Fine. I'll make sure they get it ready. Bye–bye!

Pause

Now you will hear the piece again. Rewind the tape and listen.

That is the end of the second part of the test.

THIRD PART

In the third part of the test you will hear an expert giving a listener advice about moving house. Look at question 18. Tick each piece of advice that you hear the expert give. The first one has been done for you. You will hear the piece twice.

Pause
Tone

Presenter:	The next question comes from Ann in London.
	She writes, 'I am married with two young children. We are due to move to a new house in Oxford in September. My husband thinks it will be expensive to use a removal firm and says we can hire a van to do it ourselves. What do you think? Do you have any advice? I'm worried about the move.' Well, Susan . . .
Susan:	Yes, when my husband and I moved for the first time just after we were married, the new house was just around the corner, so we decided to do it ourselves. We hired a large van but I can tell you, never again. We had to make twice as many trips as we thought! Some of the furniture didn't fit so we had to take it apart and the whole move took ages. We didn't finish till midnight and we were exhausted for days afterwards . . . It was just as well we didn't have any young children at the time! No Ann, I would really suggest that you use a removal firm.
Presenter:	Do they end up being very expensive?
Susan:	No, not really. Obviously it depends on the distance and the amount of furniture and personal belongings that you have but on the whole many removal firms are very reasonable considering the effort you save. I suggest that you get three estimates or quotes, as prices do vary, and you should make sure that you get a reputable firm that will look after your things, have proper insurance and so on . . . Also there are ways of saving money. For example it is cheaper to move during the week, so, discuss your needs with the firm you choose . . .
Presenter:	You've moved a few times now. Can you give Ann any ideas on how to overcome the main problems?
Susan:	Well, moving's not as bad as people make out, and you've got plenty of time from now till September. The most important thing is planning, so make a calendar or checklist for your move. As soon as you have a date for your move you should get an estimate from three firms. Make sure the firm's insurance covers your belongings and if you can afford it get the firm to pack for you. It often doesn't cost much more and you won't have to spend weeks packing little boxes yourself . . .
Presenter:	I'm always terrified of forgetting to do something . . .
Susan:	Yes, there are a few things to remember.
	Before the move you need to make sure that they come to read the gas and electricity meters on the morning you move. Arrange to get a bill for the telephone and make sure that you have gas, water, electricity and telephone connected at your new home. Remember too that you may need to have the washing machine and cooker disconnected, so make the arrangements as soon as you have a definite moving date and check the week before. You may also want the Post Office to redirect your mail and you can do this by asking for form RD V 15 at your local post office. It's quite easy if you make a list.
Presenter:	What about packing? I hate it.
	Yes . . . it is a lot easier if you get the movers to pack for you. If you do they'll do everything and you just need to give them room to work. If you do it yourself, most firms will lend you tea chests and boxes but it is a good idea to collect

strong cartons from your supermarket so that you can start well before the day you move. Use towels and small items of clothing to make sure fragile items don't move about and don't fill whole boxes with heavy things like books as they become very difficult to move. Make sure that things which you'll need immediately aren't packed away, and the golden rule is not to pack your tea pot, kettle, milk and cups at all as you'll need them all day. If possible try and get someone to look after your children for the day . . .

Presenter: And the day itself?

Susan: Well, there's a lot to do, so keep calm. You'll need to clean up and vacuum before you leave so make sure your cleaning materials are not packed. You may need to collect or deliver keys so make sure your solicitor and estate agent know what's happening. Your removal men will help you as they'll have done it all before. Just keep calm and save some energy to unpack essential things when you arrive. So I think the answer is Ann, get as much help as you can afford.

Pause

Now you will hear the piece again. Rewind the tape and listen.

That is the end of the third part of the test. There will now be a pause to allow you to check your work.

Pause

Tone

That is the end of the test.

PAPER 5   INTERVIEW   (15 to 20 minutes)

SECTION B   PASSAGES FOR COMMENT

Suggested answers:

1   a) Written or spoken
    b) Somebody writing for a journal or broadcasting a documentary-type programme on television or radio
    c) It gives information from a report on road accidents.

2   a) Spoken
    b) Somebody giving a talk before a live audience or on the radio
    c) The speaker is giving his/her opinion on cars as a means of transport.

3   a) Spoken or written (as in formal letter)
    b) Somebody who has just moved to London and is speaking or writing to a friend
    c) The speaker is saying how pleased he/she is not to have to commute to work by train any more.

See Introduction for marking criteria for Interview paper.

Total = 30 marks   Pass = about 18 marks